MW01181644

Conversations with Blanchie

A Novel by
Mark F. Wise

Aug 2014

To Malachi;

I hope you enjoy "Blanchie!"

Your friend,

Mark F. Wise

ISBN: 061597449X
ISBN 13: 978-0615974491
Library of Congress Control Number: 2014907588
Conversations with Blanchie, Fort Huachuca, AZ

Introduction

Dear friends,

Welcome to "Conversations with Blanchie" (referred to hereafter as 'Blanchie')! Welcome also to a part of me: a part that, all my life, has dealt with so many questions about the origin of our universe, our earth, the world's religions, our purpose on this earth, and the "afterlife."

The core of "Blanchie" is the questions posed in the chapters entitled, "Blanchie Starts to Tackle Issues" and "Bob and Blanchie Continue Discussing Core Issues."

These questions are the "elephant in the room" that most people don't want to talk about because they are controversial and, for the most part, impossible to explain, and thus taken "on faith" or just ignored. I think that most people feel that they are doubting their religions if they discuss or try to find the answers.

I am no different than you; I'm sure that you have had the same questions that are outlined in this book all your life and probably others that I have not thought of. Here, these questions are posed in a (hopefully) interesting form— that is, the basic story line of "Blanchie." You will soon realize that "Blanchie" is loosely written from a Catholic perspective, mostly because I must have some basis/perspective from which to write and grew up Roman Catholic.

I also decided to tread lightly on the scientific and religious aspects of evolutionism (the big bang theory) and creationism (God created the world in six days), as all this is so controversial, difficult to address, and best left to the thought and discussion processes that I advocate in "Blanchie."

"Blanchie" is neither a theological nor a scientific work, and I think that delving more into these aspects would have been too confusing, distracting, and downright difficult. I have tried to keep "Blanchie" simple, so each reader can reflect on each theme/question more easily.

To be clear: I am not against religion in general or any specific religion, nor am I doubting evolution or creationism. In "Blanchie," I ask the same questions that you and I and all of humankind have asked all our lives, regardless of our religion or lack thereof. Again, the main purpose of "Blanchie" is not to answer these questions but to stimulate thought and conversation on them, as, again, specified in the chapters entitled "Blanchie Starts to Tackle Issues" and "Bob and Blanchie Continue Discussing Core Issues."

You will see that Blanchie (the book character) cannot answer most of the questions, but she does her best to find the answers: the exact same thing all of us should be doing every day of our lives, either from religious or secular/scientific perspectives. Whatever perspective you choose, "Blanchie" is meant to invite a healthy discussion and thought process about these core questions.

"Blanchie" is 90 percent autobiographical, to include where it takes place, San Luis Obispo (SLO), California—one of my two hometowns (the other being Santa Barbara, California). Cuesta Park in SLO serves as the inspiration for the park that is so central to "Blanchie."

My sincerest thanks to Ms. Loretta Lopez, my writer friend, who "told it like it was" in painstakingly editing "the heck" out of "Blanchie"! Loretta, thank you for your expertise, attention to detail, and your belief in me and "Blanchie"!

My thanks also go out to my daughter, Alyssa (the inspiration for and the real life 'Honey Bunches' in the book), who also encouraged me, helped to edit "Blanchie," and, from a family member's perspective, recognized "Blanchie's" significance and potential!

Many thanks also to my wife, Tina; my son, Tim (Timothy in "Blanchie"); his wife, Krista; and their canine daughter, Roxie, for their constant moral support and encouragement.

I hope you enjoy "Blanchie," and I welcome your feedback at: conversationswithblanchie@hotmail.com.

Lastly, I dedicate "Conversations with Blanchie" to my late and dearest mother, Kathryn Claire "Speeder" Wise, the inspiration for Blanchie and Speeder, Hall of Fame single mother, grandmother, great-grandmother, daughter, and my all-time hero. Speeder, I love you so much; save a seat for me! ¡Te quiero tanto, apártame un asiento!

Sincerely,

Mark F. Wise
Cuernavaca, Mexico, and Fort Huachuca, Arizona
April 2014

Who's Who

Bob Fisher..............................Married to Blanchie for seventy-one years

Blanchie Tate Fisher ....Bob's wife

Timothy Fisher/Martha ....son/daughter-in-law

Johnny Norbert Fisher/Marie.....................son/daughter-in-law

Mary Fisher Wisniewski (Honey Bunches)/Roy......daughter/son-in-law

Bobby Jr..son who died via stillbirth

Stephan "Stevie" Kevin................................son who died at age fourteen

Charlie and Sallie Tate ....Blanchie's parents

Tessa "Speeder" Fisher ....Bob's mother

Grammie Mary "Poke" Fisher ....Bob's maternal grandmother

Carl Fisher............. Bob's German maternal grandfather who died at sea when Speeder was two years old

James Fisher...Bob's estranged father

Alyssa, Tina, Trevor.........................grandchildren (Timothy and Martha)

Hanna, Carolyn, Patrick, Melissa.........grandchildren (Johnny and Marie)

Michelle, Krista, Trevor, Brian ....grandchildren (Mary and Roy)

Tory, Kerry, Lilly, Mark, Scott, Paul, Susie, Nancy.....great-grandchildren

Father Chuck.................Parish priest, Old Mission, San Luis Obispo, CA

Park Bench.............In Cuesta Park, San Luis Obispo, CA. Bob and Blanchie sat there every morning for seventy-one years, discussing everything under the sun, especially the afterlife issues that this novel is based on.

Chapters

one

Bob and Blanchie's Early Days

*This seventy-one-year-old love affair began at the begin-
ning of World War II, the result of a happenstance encoun-
ter between two barely twenty-year-olds in Sycamore-laden
Cuesta Park in San Luis Obispo, California. I supposed one
could also say that it ended there. Do you believe in love
at first sight?*

"You know, honey, to the average person, this is probably any old
bench; it might even be invisible to them. For me, it has been the single
most special part of my life because it has been such a part of us! On
this very bench, in Cuesta Park, just four blocks from our house, I've
fallen in love with you every day for the last seventy-one years, including
this morning!

"On this bench, yesterday morning, we had our last chat together on
this earth, and this morning you went to Heaven!

"Did you ever think of what our lives would be like if we hadn't met
at this very bench that January morning, 1941? I remember you were
reading a book. You were so cute that I decided to stop and tie my shoes
on the same bench—shoes that, truth be told, in no way needed to be
tied! We made small talk, but I wasn't listening to a word you were saying, as I was trying to muster the courage to ask you for your telephone
number. Then, somehow, I did, and when you gave it to me, I specifically
remember you told me not to call after eight p.m., as that was when your
dad always arrived home from work. You said you loved him but that
he was rather 'square' when it came to dating. Then, I think I recall you
asking me, 'Hey, shoe tyer, what's your name?'

1

"Everything was such a blur, as I was in shock that you even acknowledged my presence, and then actually gave me your telephone number. I guess I must have answered, 'Bob Fisher.'

"I remember you extending your hand and offering, 'I'm Blanche, Blanche Tate, but my friends call me Blanchie.'

"'Blanche…Isn't that something they do to vegetables or something?'

"'Well, yes, silly Bob—except it's spelled without an *e* at the end!'

"'Does this mean I'm in hot water for asking?'

"Remember how we laughed for a good five minutes, until we both cried? Passersby must have thought we had lost our marbles! I can still feel how happy it made me when you called me 'silly Bob,' kinda like being back in third grade!

"Our first date: Laurel Lanes on Laurel Avenue four days later. Remember how you laughed when I called you and asked if you would like to go…in your 'spare' time? Well, okay, it took you a second to get it, and then you added, 'Sure, bowling is right up my alley!' I think at that precise moment I knew who I wanted to spend the rest of my life with!

"I also think you deserve a medal for putting up with my puns all these years! Well, okay, maybe even a Purple Heart!

"Honey, as I recall, our first date was at Laurel Lanes and was awkward but exciting at the same time. I remember ordering two malteds at the snack bar, but the girl behind the counter winked at me as she handed me one malted with two straws. I thought this was odd, but I somehow didn't tell her she had made a mistake. Even though we timed our sips so each one sipped 'at a safe distance,' remember how we then took a sip at the same time and how our faces and lips came 'dangerously close'? It didn't seem to bother you, and God knows I was in seventh heaven!

"And, remember, Blanchie, how we saw each other every day for the next few weeks, never with any real agenda, especially since neither of us had money, a car, or even a bicycle? I recall us walking downtown to see matinees at the Obispo and Fremont theaters, and other times just window shopping; all the while I was too chicken to hold your hand! And, yes, we often went to 'our park' and sat on 'our bench,' remember? It was perfect; each time I left you at your door, I couldn't wait to see you again. I remember so many nights tossing and turning in my bed, just seeing your face, your smile, and your inviting lips, hearing your laughter…heck, all this kept me awake! There was no getting around it—you were the 'cat's meow' then and always have been!

"Friday, February 14, 1941—do you remember why that day is so special? Yes, I know I've told you a million times! It's the day I finally summoned up the courage to kiss you for the first time—on this very bench! The day before, I thought, okay, tomorrow is St. Valentine's Day; what better day?

"We were twenty-one years young, and I didn't sleep the night before! I had planned this out in every detail and wanted it to come off to perfection! I hadn't counted on my pores opening up all at once, or so it seemed. I could feel the moisture beading on my face, and my palms were getting sweaty. Even in the crisp fall air, I hadn't counted on my woolen pants sticking to my legs as we walked toward our bench, or my freshly starched shirt adhering to my chest and arms.

"I was a basket case! What if you pulled away or said no or…

"I can still feel your soft lips and the tingle that ran from the top of my spine down to my toes! And I remember how your eyes sparkled as we both opened our eyes at the same time! And your perfume—it melted me then, and it has continued to do so all these years!

"Sunday, December 14, 1941—a week after the invasion of Pearl Harbor and the day my draft notice arrived. My orders said to report to the Military Entrance Processing Station three days later in downtown SLO. We were sitting on this very bench, my hands shaking as I awkwardly placed the small box with my grandmother's wedding ring in your hands.

"I was so nervous! What if you pulled away or said no or, worse yet, said yes? Even though I forgot to even pop the question, I still remember your response:

"'Yes, yes, yes, yes, silly Bob! You haven't asked, but yes, of course I'll marry you! What a silly unasked question! What took you so long? Oh, my goodness, Bob, that *is* what you were trying to ask me, right?'

"As I recall, at that moment we both laughed nervously and instinctively stood up very slowly. I then gently placed my arms around your waist, and, gazing into your sparkling hazel eyes, I gently kissed your beautiful red lips ever so slowly. I think this was our first long kiss!

"Seventy-one years of incredible happiness that blessed us with Johnny, Timothy, Mary, Bobby, and Stevie!

"Blanchie, you will always be my best friend and my rock, and I ask you to help me get through this tough time before I see you again in Heaven! The highlight of my day, every day, throughout these seventy-one years, was sitting here with you every morning before work from seven to eight a.m., sipping our coffee and talking about the kids, grandkids, great-grandkids, world events, the economy, and politics. Of course, our most favorite topics over the years have always dealt with worldwide religions, evolution versus creationism, the proverbial meaning of life, and, our favorite, to borrow from *Let's Make a Deal*, what's beyond door number three: the 'afterlife.'

"Seventy-one years of a habit are hard to break, so, I guess, I'll still get us moving in the morning with my usual proclamation: 'Blanchie, our bench awaiteth. Grab your coffee!'

"My dearest Blanchie, this morning your soul left this earth, but I continue to feel your spirit next to me on this bench! It's a very odd—even surreal—feeling! As long as God lets me, I will continue to sit on this bench, so I can at least feel your presence!

"I love you so very much…and oh, how I miss you already!"

two

The Kids Arrive at the Bench

"By the way, Blanchie, Johnny, Timothy, and Mary arrived this morning and are here at home helping in so many ways, most importantly with your obit, the plans for the mass and wake in our living room in two days and our final good-bye the morning after at the Old Mission mass and burial at the Catholic Cemetery.

"Okay, speaking of which, I see the kids are walking over here toward us. I guess they knew where I, or maybe I should say *we*, would be!

"Johnny! Timothy! Honey Bunches! Come sit with your mother and me! Now, don't look at each other like that! I know it sounds crazy, but I can feel Mom…I know she's with us, right here, right now…Come and sit, and you'll feel her presence, too!"

Bob's three children then quietly join him on the bench, each gently kissing him on the forehead. After about sixty seconds, Mary breaks the awkward silence, looks upward, and, in a broken voice, ekes out a barely audible, "I love you, Mom," followed by Timothy and Johnny. At that instant, they spontaneously break out in tears and form a group hug.

"Let's just sit here, the five of us, just like we did so many times as you grew up, on this bench and at the kitchen table. Remember, kids, over the years, our precious times sitting together that ranged from reading Dr. Seuss, reviewing the times tables, discussing boyfriend and girlfriend issues, and, yes, speculating on those millions of religious and life topics that Mom and I so much liked to discuss?

"Mom and I so enjoyed discussing these questions with you, especially since Father Chuck didn't. He would always find a reason to not directly answer them, mostly by telling Mom and me, 'You just have to take these issues on faith; someday we will all know the answers.'

"You know, all three of you have provided us with maybe most of the religious topics that Mom and I discussed over the years; remember, from the most childlike topics in grammar school to those that seemed to be at the theological doctoral level when you were in high school and college?

"Honey Bunches, I guess you were about five years old…do you remember, we were sitting at the dining room table eating dinner, when out of the blue, you blurted: 'Mommy and Daddy, what's the temperature in Heaven?' You were so cute!"

"Yes, Dad, I think I remember! Didn't Mom answer with something like, 'Honey Bunches, I'm not sure, but I'll try to find out, okay?'

"Dad, why don't we head back to the house and Johnny, Timothy, and I will make dinner!"

"Sounds like a plan! Here, help this old geezer up, okay?"

"By the way, Blanchie, if you can hear me, what is the temperature in Heaven?"

three

Blanchie Responds, Day 3

"Good morning, Blanchie, here I am again. This is day two since you went to Heaven. I just wanted—"

"My dearest Bob, I am fine, and I, too, love you and miss you! Yes, as you said yesterday, I am right here with you, on our bench!"

"Blanchie? Blanchie? Is, is…is that…is that…you? Am I hearing you in my head, or have I lost my marbles, or both? What is going on?"

"Oh, silly Bob! Don't ask me how, but I think I'm right next to you on our bench! It appears that you can hear me, but you can't see me! I'm just as surprised as you, and I don't understand, either!

"Okay, just to test this, who was my all-time favorite LA Dodger pitcher that we saw so many times at Dodger Stadium? And how many times did we go to Dodger Stadium over the years? Oh, yeah, who went with us on those fun bus trips to Dodger Stadium?"

"Uh, Blanchie, well, I guess Sandy Koufax was your all-time favorite Dodger? Who know knows how many times we went to Dodger Stadium, but I wish I had a penny for each time that we went! Lastly, it was Father Chuck who went with us on those great bus trips to Dodger Stadium!"

"Bob…You said Sandy Koufax! You also said you wished you had a penny for each time we went to Dodger Stadium and that it was Father Chuck who went with us on those fun bus trips!"

"It's working, Blanchie! It's working! I can't believe it!"

"Oh, Bob, I can't believe it, either! Don't ask me what's going on! Let me say that I am very happy, and I'm in that incredibly beautiful and special place that we speculated on every day of our lives from this very bench: I'm in Heaven!"

"I knew it, Blanchie. I knew it! Whoo-hoo!"

"I seem to be in a sort of 'reception' area that looks strangely like the Old Mission's multipurpose room where we always had coffee and donuts after mass! They say I'll soon have a week of orientation classes about what's going on and what the future will hold!

"Oh, Bob, I'm so confused!

"I agree with everything that you said! What a life we had on Earth, and how blessed we were! For me, too, the highlight of each day and the highlight of my life were the daily conversations on our bench before we went to work! I think there wasn't a subject we didn't discuss, especially as related to Earth and the afterlife!

"Oh, and about your puns, Bob—I agree about the Purple Heart! Speaking of your lifelong obsession with puns, do you remember your first one—you know, the first of who knows how many times during those seventy-one years, with which we started our hour of conversations?"

"I sure do, Blanchie, and remember how you asked me to start our daily conversations with, 'Bob, would you please say grace?'

"Yes, my memory is crystal clear! My first grace—I mean, pun—was actually a combined effort between you and me! I said, 'Blanchie, did you hear about the dog's master who threw a stick clear across the park?' Then you answered, 'No, Bob, I didn't, but it sounds so farfetched!'

"Ah, yes, Bob, I do remember!"

"I think we never laughed so hard!"

"Oh, silly Bob, stop it already; I'm splitting a gut seventy-one years later! Please open our daily conversations again the same way, okay?"

"Sure, Blanchie! Remember what Jimmy Durante used to say: 'I got a million of 'em!'"

"My dearest Bob, I remember the day we met. It was Saturday, January 11, 1941—such an important day in our lives! As you slowly approached the bench, you seemed somewhat confused or indecisive. I remember thinking to myself, 'What in the world is this guy going to do? He's tying his shoes right next to me? Oh my God, do I say something?' I saw how you glanced at me from the corner of your right eye, and I was so relieved when you started to talk! Your voice was sweet, even as you commented on the pretty 'cumulus clouds'! Not really the most interesting subject, but it broke the ice!"

"I thought you were quite fetching, no pun intended! Oh, Blanchie, I spotted you about one hundred feet away, and my knees immediately turned to jelly. And my hands? Shaking like leaves in a storm! You were the prettiest girl I had ever laid eyes on!"

"Well, Mr. Jelly, it's a good thing you didn't hear what I was saying, too, as I'm sure I dribbled on and on about God knows what. I, too, was so nervous! I remember you asked me for my phone number, so you could let me know when *Little Town on the Prairie* would be available at Dryer's Bookstore, where you worked. I thought that was so cute—and very clever! Then I worried that you'd forget the number, as neither of us carried anything to write with or to write on!

"Two days later I was never as surprised or happy as when you called me! Luckily I answered the phone; you called at eight thirty p.m., thirty minutes after Dad got home, instead of before eight as I had told you. I remember you said, 'Uh, hi, uh, this is, uh, Bob, Bob Fisher. Uh, is this, uh, we met at Cuesta Park two days ago.'"

"Ha, yes, Blanchie, as embarrassing as it was, I do remember! Boy, was I nervous!"

"You were so cute! And yes, I remember you asking, rather awkwardly, if I would like to go bowling in my 'spare' time! You always claimed that you didn't say this on purpose? Ha! I still find that hard to believe! Well, I'll tell you that my response was on purpose: 'Oh, yes, bowling is right up my alley!' Yes, at that point, I think I, too, knew that we had clicked and that you were the one for me!

"Yes, Johnny, Timothy, Bobby Jr, Stevie, and Mary—our pride and joy! They gave us so much to be thankful for! I love and miss them so!"

"I think I'll hold off on saying anything to the kids about our conversations, as I've already gotten some odd looks from some of the people passing by. They probably think that I'm talking to an imaginary friend and wondering where my bottle of Ripple or Mad Dog is!"

"Bob, there's something I told you from time to time, but I never told you enough: how proud I am, or, maybe now I should say *was*, of you as my husband and our children's father. You were, and are, without a doubt, the very best wood engraver artisan and scientific book illustrator that the world has known! The fact that you never have received the attention you have deserved speaks to your passion for your work, and not the notoriety that most people with lesser talents have strived for, all at the expense of their marriages and parenthood.

"Honey, if I had to do it over again, a thousand times I would marry you! We made a great team together, and it looks like we'll continue to, also, even if only from our bench! We didn't have glamorous professions, especially me, as a retired high school librarian, but we were happy, weren't we? And then our children, grandchildren, and great-grandchildren made our lives so much happier, interesting, and full! In this aspect, the most important one, we were billionaires!"

"Oh, Blanchie, I can't wait to join you and continue our life, or, I guess, our 'afterlife' together! Right now, we're all focused on the tasks at hand: your wake tomorrow and the funeral mass and your burial at the Catholic Cemetery the day after...now does *that* sound odd?"

"I know, Bob, and, yes, it does sound so very odd! So, tomorrow is my wake, and in our own living room! This is just as we had always talked about: where my Grandpa Johnny and Grandma Mary were waked, too!

"Good night, Bob! Well, what do I say here, 'see you in the morning'? This is so weird! I love you so much!"

"Yes, Blanchie, this *is* so weird! As Honey Bunches used to say, "Whoodathunk?'

"I love you too and I have so many questions—mostly the ones we talked about for so many years on this very bench! I guess at this point I should say 'I'll hear you in the morning!'"

four

Blanchie's Death

"Uh, good morning, Blanchie, are you, are you…"

"Yes, dear, I'm here, right next to you, and I have my coffee with me! By the way, I'll explain about the coffee in Heaven later! Remember how we used to say, 'This coffee tastes just heavenly'?

"Oh, just a thought, but you said the passersby are seeing you talk to seemingly no one? I don't want anyone putting you in a straitjacket and hauling you off to the 'funny farm'!"

"You know, Blanchie, that's a very good point! I'll either have to look around me and make sure I'm alone before I speak, or borrow one of the kids'…what are they called…smart phones and pretend that I'm talking to someone!"

"Say, Bob, I suppose at some point we'd have to talk about this, so better sooner than later. You must be wondering what my death was like for me and what my 'crossing over to the other side' was also like. For that somber reason, I think we can skip the 'grace' this morning!

"I guess I was lucky in that I 'died in my sleep,' as is often said. I think I overheard the coroner say it was a stroke. I don't remember feeling any pain. Actually, I don't remember anything about the moment when I guess I died, but I do remember most everything after.

"My poor Bob, at six thirty a.m. you tried to wake me for us to grab our coffee and go sit on our bench. I remember the smell of coffee in the air!

"I could hear you call me from the kitchen downstairs. When I didn't respond, I then felt you gently shaking me on the shoulder. You were sobbing, and in a broken voice, you said 'Blanchie, time to get up. C'mon, you know…our bench…awaiteth! C'mon, Blanchie, you know…our bench awaiteth!'

"You must have suspected that something was wrong, because I always got up before you and made the coffee. Then I heard you say, 'Oh, no, no, no, Blanchie, not today, please, not today, no, God, no, not today! I'm not ready! Just give me one more day with my Blanchie; I beg you! Just one more day! My Blanchie! I love you so!'

"You were hysterical! I heard you fumble with the phone, then drop it before you finally called Johnny, who I suppose called 911. I then could feel you lie down next to me, sobbing as you stroked my hair in silence, until the paramedics knocked on the front door and you let them in. I so wanted to comfort you, but I felt helpless, as if my hands were tied and my mouth bound."

"Oh, Blanchie, I was hysterical and panicked! I guess we both felt helpless! It was pure torture watching the paramedics doing those chest compressions and mouth-to-mouth with one of those plastic devices, not knowing if I had lost you or not. My heart totally sank when one of the paramedics stopped administering the CPR, looked at his watch, and announced, 'I'm so sorry, Mr. Fisher. We've lost Mrs. Fisher. Time of death, zero six forty-seven.'"

"Oh, my dearest Bob, I saw you fall to your knees, supporting yourself on the bed, at the exact moment that Johnny entered our bedroom. He fell to his knees next to you, too, both of you sobbing. In a moment that you and Johnny didn't know we were all sharing, I felt helpless and so wanted to tell both of you not to cry, that I was okay! But who was going to tell me not to cry?

"I was very touched when Johnny helped you up and you kissed my forehead, and then when he did the same! I remember you whispering in my ear, 'Blanchie, save a seat for me on our bench in Heaven!' Well, Bob, I did!

"And Johnny touched me very deeply, too, when his voice quivered and he said, 'I love you, Mom. Have a great journey, and we'll see each other before too long!'

"I so wanted to tell you both that, *really*, I was fine!"

"My dear, dear Blanchie, it's so surreal to hear you say all this, but comforting at the same time! We had always talked about how one of us would feel if the other one died. I feel comforted that you were able to feel our love and that you did not suffer! The good thing is that you did not die alone, which is something you and I discussed so many times on our bench! I love you so much!"

"And so do I, Bob! And, yes, all of this is so surreal! Just think about it…you and I are discussing my wake at home tomorrow, followed by the funeral mass and burial the day after!

"Bob, there are so many things about Heaven that I don't know, and I'm anxious to start finding out the answers to all our questions over the years. Right now, I get most of my answers from fellow 'residents,' so to speak! It's all kind of overwhelming, but imagine how it would be for both of us if we were not able to talk like this! This is all so taxing on my emotions; what say we take a break until tomorrow morning?"

"I agree, honey; I think you and I are pretty much basket cases at this point! Just know how much I love you!"

"Silly Bob, I love you too! At some point I'll explain the details of my experiences so far, like where I live now and who I've seen—things like that. Talk to you tomorrow!"

five

A Good Old-Fashioned Irish Wake

"My dearest Blanchie, good morning! For some reason this morning, my knees had trouble lowering this ole geezer's posterior onto our bench while balancing my coffee! Guess I'm thinking about today's mass and wake and feeling a bit stressed! Do you mind if I don't say grace again?"

"Good morning, Bob, I'm right here with you, and, no, I don't mind if we skip the grace! These are difficult times for you and me, as well as for everyone else."

"I asked the kids to come and get me just before the hearse arrives from Rice Funeral Home; they should be arriving any second. The kids have been great, arranging for everything *a* to *z*, from notifying Father Chuck and the guests to creating your obit, to arranging for the food to be catered from Muzio's and then setting everything up with Rice to bring your earthly body back home, so that your family and friends can say good-bye to you in our home. Now how weird does all that sound?

"And, Blanchie, as soon as the obit is finished, I'll read it to you!

"So many times we discussed how each of us wanted to be waked in our living room, just like my mother's Irish-American grandfather and grandmother.

"By the way, Blanchie, don't think that I have in any way adjusted to your passing; it's just that all these events have to happen very quickly, and, thankfully, Johnny, Honey Bunches, and Timothy have been able to handle them! I pray for God's strength that I make it through the rest of today's and tomorrow's events! What say you and I help each other, too?"

"Bob, I agree with you! Please, please tell everyone not to be sad—that I am in a wonderful place, a place that our faith has always reminded us is pure happiness! I can't wait to greet you here when you arrive!"

"Hey, Blanchie, do you know something that I don't?"

"Silly Bob, I'll keep you guessing! I also ask you to relay my love to Johnny, Timothy, and Mary in your own way. Tell them that I love and miss them and that we'll all be together soon for all eternity!"

"Blanchie, they know that you love them! I think I'll tell them about our continued conversations at the right time. They are overwhelmed right now, and the fact that you and I are communicating directly would, I'm sure, confuse them.

"Well, honey, it's ten a.m., and Mary is walking toward me. I'm sure she's going to tell me that your casket is soon to arrive from Rice's. This sounds so odd to say, but I'll see you in a few minutes!"

As Mary slowly approaches her father, he can easily see her swollen red eyes. This is a sad and awkward moment for both of them. What does one say or do at a moment like this?

"Honey Bunches, come sit with me and Mom! I can feel her presence; come say something to her! Oh, and here's a Kleenex. I can see that you could use one. Lord knows I've gone through a few boxes already! I understand your tears; I guess we're all basket cases!"

Without saying anything, Mary kisses her father on the forehead and slowly sits next to him. As they both sit on the bench in silence, Mary summons up the courage and composure before she chokes out: "Mom, if you can hear me, I love you so much, and I miss you so!"

"Bob, please tell Mary at the appropriate time that I heard her and that I love her so much!"

"Honey Bunches, I'm sure that Mom heard you and that she, too, is telling you that she loves and misses you so much!"

"You think so, Dad? I'm sure you're right!"

The four blocks back to the house from the bench were the longest and most dreaded four blocks of Bob's life! Despite Blanchie's request to not be sad, his eyes

*instinctively welled up with tears, and his knees wanted
to buckle as Mary and he approached the house.*

"Dad, I know this is hardest for you and Johnny. Timothy and I
are here to support you, to share in our grief and in celebrating Mom's
life."

"Thanks, Honey Bunches. The wake will be the toughest event of
my life, but I'll have to get through it, as we all will!"

"Dad, don't forget that this will be an Irish wake, so there will be a
little of everything, from crying to knee-slapping laughter. You'll see!
There will be a lot of beautiful stories about Mom! It will be a great
afternoon and evening!"

"Thanks, Honey Bunches. You have always been such a sensitive and
comforting child and adult!"

*As Mary and Bob arrived at the house, the hearse was
backing into the driveway. There to serve as pallbearers
and carry their grandmother and great-grandmother were
Michael, Timothy, Mark, Sutton, Kevin, Trevor, Brian, and
Scott.*

*Johnny, Timothy, Mary, and Bob, along with grand-
daughters Alyssa, Hanna, Tessa, Melissa, and Michelle,
formed a kind of impromptu path, down which Blanchie
would be carried, then up the front steps into the living
room.*

*Bob seemed to not be prepared for the pallbearers to so
solemnly back the casket out of the hearse and, with the
guidance of the funeral staff, gently place the casket on top
of the wheeled support device in the living room in front
of the fireplace.*

*Seventy-one years of love and happiness—Bob was ask-
ing himself why he was not focusing on that instead of
sobbing so selfishly and uncontrollably?*

"Blanchie, I'm sorry, I know you said not to be sad, but I can't help
it. I'm losing my lifelong best friend and my rock!"

*An Irish wake is like an open house; people come and
go as they please. The kids planned for Father Chuck from
the Old Mission to say mass at 6:00 p.m. in the living room,*

followed by an unrehearsed "open mic" session at seven for anyone to say whatever they pleased as they ate catered food.

Father Chuck spoke in down-to-earth terms about Blanchie, whom he had known for the forty years that he had been at the Old Mission. Like Blanchie and me, Father Chuck was a die-hard LA Dodger fan, and his sermons often included baseball analogies. Blanchie's eulogy was no different.

"Blanche knew the Lord, as do her children, their children, and their children's children, thanks to Blanche's and Bob's faith and devotion over the years. She was a 'Hall of Fame' wife, mother, grandmother, and great-grandmother! I'm sure she was immediately inducted into this heavenly Hall of Fame four days ago on her first eligibility! Blanche, you were this family's most valuable player!"

As mass ended, Father Chuck invited everyone to serve themselves food from the dining room, and at the same time encouraged all to say whatever they wanted, to honor Blanchie.

No one got up to get food. After what seemed to be an eternity of silence, Bob nodded at Johnny, and he helped Bob up from his chair. It seemed to be Bob's unofficial 'duty' to be the first to speak during the "open mic" session of the wake. Completely forgetting what Blanchie had told him, he tearfully directed his words to Blanchie in her casket in a halting and broken voice. Staring lovingly at Blanchie and touching her casket, he said:

"My dearest Blanchie, I know you also believed in love at first sight, because it happened to both of us seventy-one years ago on our bench, just four blocks from here!

"Everyone here knows our story, how we began and the overwhelming 'ups' in our life as compared to the very few 'downs.' My dearest Blanchie, maybe my biggest regret is not having been able to give you and our kids a better life financially. Thank you for loving and supporting me all these years, and for giving us and this world our swell kids, Johnny, Timothy, Mary, Bobby, and Stevie.

"Blanchie, I'm sure that Stevie and Bobby Jr. are at your side as we speak! Throughout the years since we lost them, there hasn't been a minute of every waking hour that I haven't thought of them and how much I love them! Please tell them this and that Johnny, Timothy, and Mary also send their love.

"Thank you, Blanchie, for being my soul mate, my best friend and debater, as well as a Hall of Fame wife, mother, grandmother, and great-grandmother! I love you so!"

Johnny led his father back to his chair, then stood next to his mother's casket and spoke these words to her:

"Mom, this is Johnny. I'm so glad you wanted an Irish wake, as it gives all of us the chance to personally thank you, honor you, and yes, say good-bye in our most comfortable and familiar setting! And, oh, well, maybe also to roast you a little, if you don't mind!

"Mom, I love you! Dad and Father Chuck said it best: you are a Hall of Fame mother!

"I am what I am because of you and Dad. You did your jobs as parents superbly, loving us unconditionally and preparing us for living in this world as good Christians, citizens, spouses, and parents. This is all one can ask of their parents and all we can ask of ourselves as parents, too!

"Now, talking to some of your childhood friends this afternoon, I learned a few things out about my 'perfect' mom! Okay, let's see a show of hands here of those who knew that Mom, at eight years of age, played 'Holy Communion' with Jimmy Mahoney, using Necco wafer candies? Ha, I knew it! Father Chuck, was this blasphemous, and do you think it affected Mom's induction into the 'Heavenly Hall of Fame'?"

"Well, Johnny, let me see...I'll have to get back to you!"

"Mom, you also instilled other critically important virtues and life skills in me: a good sense of humor, a hard work ethic, compassion, tolerance, common sense, and a real nose for a good rummage sale bargain down at the Vets Hall!

"I remember when you made all of us memorize Max Ehrmann's poem *Desiderata,* which you said summed up everything a person should know, do, and be in life. If everyone would please indulge me while I read it:

Go placidly amid the noise and the haste,
and remember what peace there may be in silence.
As far as possible, without surrender,
be on good terms with all persons.
Speak your truth quietly and clearly;
and listen to others,
even to the dull and the ignorant;
they too have their story.
Avoid loud and aggressive persons;
they are vexatious to the spirit.
If you compare yourself with others,
you may become vain or bitter,
for always there will be greater and lesser persons than yourself.
Enjoy your achievements as well as your plans.
Keep interested in your own career, however humble;
it is a real possession in the changing fortunes of time.
Exercise caution in your business affairs,
for the world is full of trickery.
But let this not blind you to what virtue there is;
many persons strive for high ideals,
and everywhere life is full of heroism.
Be yourself. Especially do not feign affection.
Neither be cynical about love,
for in the face of all aridity and disenchantment,
it is as perennial as the grass.
Take kindly the counsel of the years,
gracefully surrendering the things of youth.
Nurture strength of spirit to shield you in sudden misfortune.
But do not distress yourself with dark imaginings.
Many fears are born of fatigue and loneliness.
Beyond a wholesome discipline, be gentle with yourself.
You are a child of the universe
no less than the trees and the stars;
you have a right to be here.
And whether or not it is clear to you,
no doubt the universe is unfolding as it should.

Therefore be at peace with God,
whatever you conceive Him to be.
And whatever your labors and aspirations,
in the noisy confusion of life,
keep peace in your soul.
With all its sham, drudgery, and broken dreams,
it is still a beautiful world.
Be cheerful. Strive to be happy.

"I love you so much, Mom!"

"Mom, this is Honey Bunches...well, there I go, getting all choked up, and I just started! Here I am, the baby of the family at sixty-four! I've always been your Honey Bunches, and I always will be! I can't add anything to what Johnny just said, and it's a good thing, 'cause I'm already a nervous wreck!

"To Mom's many friends, I want to thank you for coming out this afternoon. Each of you held a special niche in Mom's heart, and I know she loves you and is watching from above!

"Finally, Mom, before my Kleenex runs out, I want to say that I do remember asking you in the kitchen, I guess around age five, 'What is the temperature in Heaven?' This was one of my earliest memories!

"I guess now you know the answer!

"I love you so much, Mom!"

"Hi, Mom, last but not least, this is Timothy. Dad, Johnny, and Mary are tough acts to follow, but words could never express what you have meant for me, and still do. While many parents talk the talk but don't walk the walk, you did both. This is how we all have known how to act in life, by just following your example.

"Mom, I guess the only thing I could add is to ask you to say hi to Bobby, Stevie, and all my relatives on both sides that I either haven't seen in many years or have never met. For that reason, too, this must be such a joyous time for you; enjoy it! Mom, there's not a dry eye here in the living room, including your grandkids and great-grandkids!

"We all miss you and love you so very much!"

Out of the two hundred or so guests that came off and on during the day to pay their respects, about thirty were present at the eulogy, including Blanchie's closest high school friends, Mary Rizzoli, Pat Bond, Maureen Lubers, and Jimmy Mahoney, as well as current and former neighbors.

There came a point at which the atmosphere in the living room with Blanchie present was more casual, and the food was almost gone. Many of the 'rug rats,' the small children of some of the guests, started to play on the floor next to Blanchie's casket. Bob was thinking how great this was, and exactly as Blanchie would have wanted it—surrounded by children, so loving and innocent!

Johnny, Timothy, and Mary organized a vigil schedule that night for those who wanted to pray next to Blanchie for an hour at a time. Bob chose 7:00 to 8:00 a.m., the last time slot before the hearse was scheduled to arrive, and the hour when their conversations took place on the bench for so many years.

six

Our Final Earthly Good-bye to Blanchie

"My dearest Blanchie, I hope you can hear me, even if I'm not on our bench. In a few minutes, the hearse will arrive to take you to the Old Mission for mass and then to the Catholic Cemetery. Somehow I don't feel as sad as maybe I thought I would at this moment; I feel very close to you. I don't really have much more to add to what I've already said. I've just enjoying sitting next to you in silence for the past hour."

"My dearest Bob, I can feel you next to me! I witnessed the entire mass and wake and everyone that came to visit last night. Everything was so beautiful, thanks to you and the kids! Know that I will be present with you and the kids at mass and the cemetery today! I promise you one thing—that we will all be together again soon. This is what our stay on Earth and entrance into Heaven seem to be all about—I guess a kind of trial period!"

"Honey, it is such a comfort to know that we can talk anywhere, so we really don't have to say good-bye, do we? I mean, we can continue to meet at our bench or at home, and you can continue to find out the answers to our many, many questions about life and the afterlife!"

"Yes, Bob...isn't it great?"

"Uh, Blanchie, one more thing...Do you know anything about my future, well, you know..."

"Silly Bob, no, I don't know when you will die and come to Heaven! I remember, though, how we used to contemplate if, maybe, we would be the classic couple that dies within a week or so of each other."

"You know, honey, in many ways I would love us to be that couple!

22

"Well, people are starting to stir in the house. I better sign off, or they'll think I've got bats in my belfry talking to you! I love you so much!"

"I love you so much, too! Let's talk tomorrow on our bench, okay?"

"Sounds great, Blanchie! Make sure you bring your Pete's coffee!"

The house slowly comes to life, and, somehow, every-one is ready to go as the hearse pulls up at 9:00 a.m. sharp. Bob asked to ride to mass and to the Catholic Cemetery with Johnny and his family, turning down the funeral home's offer for me to ride with them. He needed to be with family and the strength that would give him.

Mass was very moving, with three of the grandkids, Alyssa, Timothy, and Hanna, doing the readings and bring-ing the hosts and wine up to the altar. During the distribu-tion of communion, Johnny's daughter, Carolyn, brought everyone to tears when she sang Blanchie's favorite hymn, "Ave Maria."

After Father Chuck gave the final blessing and mass ended, it seemed the right thing for Bob to say a few words.

"Thank you to everyone for coming to this celebration of Blanchie's life. I barely got through my words last night at the wake, so I'm not going to tempt fate again! Is there anyone who would like to say some-thing before we all head out to the Catholic Cemetery?"

No one came forward.

"I think most everyone here was at last night's mass and wake at our home, and many of you spoke at the wake. Those of you that wish to attend Blanchie's internment, please proceed to the Catholic Cemetery."

The ride to the cemetery was almost eerily silent; probably everyone was trying to prepare for their final moments with their beloved mother, grandmother, great-grandmother, friend, and, yes, wife.

The internment was simple and quick, maybe twenty minutes. The pallbearers, our grandkids, with the guidance of the funeral personnel, gently placed the casket on top of the two green straps that would electrically lower it into the ground. Father Chuck read a few Scripture passages, and at the end of the official portion of the service, he encouraged those forty or so present to gently drop their roses and a handful of dirt on top of the casket before it was lowered.

As Bob stood at the edge of the grave site, for some reason he had no more tears and felt at peace. His family waited while he stared alone into the grave with his head bowed. When he lifted his head, Mary, Johnny, Timothy, and their families gently and quietly filled the space that surrounded him. No one spoke; there was no need to. They just hugged.

As Bob and his family slowly moved away from the grave site, he sought out many of his and Blanchie's friends who seemed to be unsure if they should approach. Bob wanted to express his appreciation not just for them having come to the cemetery but for having been their friends, some for close to eighty-five years, since they were in grammar school. This was a special time for Bob, especially when he asked his entire family to come close and did a group introduction or, in some cases, a reintroduction of his friends to his family. Bob knew that this would be his last chance to share his and Blanchie's friends with his family.

The introductions and good-byes took about thirty minutes, and Bob's my tear ducts seemed to be empty. He was feeling now, more than ever, a "life-sharing" mood as he prepared to leave the cemetery. He felt the need to continue sharing his past with his grandkids and great-grandkids, things that Johnny, Mary, and Timothy had heard and seen so many times before! As if on cue, Mary then asked, "Dad, since we're all together here at the cemetery, would this be a good time to explain a little about its 'residents,' especially our relatives, before we all scatter to the four winds tomorrow? You've told us, I mean, your kids, many times, but your grandkids and great-grandkids haven't heard anything about their ancestors directly from you."

"By George, Honey Bunches, that's a great idea! Okay, kids, to start with, this is the Catholic Cemetery, where, as I'm sure you've already guessed, mostly Catholics are buried and have been for over one hundred and fifty years. When I was your age, right after fire and electricity were invented, the Protestant and Jewish cemeteries were off limits to me and Grandma Blanchie. Ah ha, Kerry, I saw your eyes roll! Of course I was joking; it was electricity that hadn't been invented yet!

"Anyway, when I was growing up, the Old Mission forbade us Catholics from attending other faiths' religious services and entering the Protestant and Jewish cemeteries across the street. Over the last thirty or so years, Grandma Blanchie and I often remarked how we were glad that times had changed to allow these things to happen nowadays!

"Okay, so right here, to the right of Grandma Blanchie's grave, is Grandma Poke's grave, my mother."

"Grandpa, that's a funny name! Why was she called Grandma Poke?"

"Ah, Tory, your Great Uncle Stevie came up with that name, but no one knows why! Anyway, you can ask him, because he's buried next to Gramma Poke, right in front of you!"

"Grandpa, how did Uncle Stevie and Uncle Bobby die?"

"Kerry, Uncle Bobby died as the result of a miscarriage at the end of the fourth month, and we never knew why, or, I should say, the doctors never knew why. There is his grave, to the left, next to Uncle Stevie. Now, Uncle Stevie died while riding his bike when he was fourteen, struck by a car here in SLO. I'm sure that your two great uncles love you very much and are watching out for you from Heaven! There's not a minute of every day that I don't think about Bobby and Stevie and tell them how much I love them!

"Okay, so next to Grammie Poke is my mother, Tessa Fisher, but everyone called her 'Speeder.' Tori and Kerry, I know you're going to ask why everyone called her 'Speeder'! Again, your funny Great Uncle Stevie gave her that nickname, I think because Grammie Speeder used to walk fast and do most things fast, even cleaning the house! The nickname just stuck!

"Kids, here is where Grandma Blanchie's parents, Charlie and Sallie Tate, are buried. They were such wonderful people, and I miss them a lot! You would have loved them, and they would have loved you so much!"

"Dad, next to Grammie Speeder is your dad, James Fisher. Were you going to talk about him?"

"Timothy, I suppose I should say something, right? Kids, my dad was just not cut out to be a father, husband, or grandfather. Growing up, he never showed me or my mother any love nor had much contact with us. I don't remember him taking us to the zoo, to the beach, or to get an ice cream—*anything*!

I vowed early on to not be like him, so let's just say that he was the opposite of what you've seen in me for as long as you've known me. I hope to be able to reconcile with him one day in Heaven."

"That's okay, Dad. Just these few minutes have been special for me as well as for your grandkids and great-grandkids, hearing a little more about their ancestors from you.

"Now, let's see a show of hands of those who would like to go to Hometown Buffet!"

"My pleasure, Honey Bunches! I wish we had time to show them some of our memories, like our high schools, the downtown area, Bishop Peak, Morro Bay, Avila Beach, and, most importantly, our bench!"

"Not to worry, Dad. They've seen your favorite memories many times. Don't forget that Johnny, Timothy, and I have always taken pride in showing our kids and grandkids all of your memories and the beautiful sites of SLO and surrounding areas. We will continue to do so, too. Right now I think you and your grandkids and great-grandkids should relax and enjoy these rare moments together with the extended family. It's been a long and emotionally draining day!"

"You're right as rain, Honey Bunches, and I could eat a horse!"

The Hometown Buffet was delicious and, as always, a favorite place to go to for Blanchie, Bob, the kids, and the "grands and greats," as they sometimes referred to them. Bob thoroughly enjoyed being with his entire extended family—something that was extra special because it was the first time we had all been together at one time. He wondered if they would all be together again.

At home, everyone changed into more comfortable clothes. Johnny, as he always had done throughout his life, made a fire in the fireplace, and everyone just sat around, listening to the fire crackle, savoring the moment and enjoying one another. At times, brief waves of sadness would enter Bob's mind because he missed Blanchie, and he knew that, in the morning, his family would be going back to their homes. It was maybe the most meaningful night of Bob's life.

"Dad, could you elaborate more on Stevie's and Bobby's passings? Your great-grandchildren here tonight are all old enough, and I thought that all of us should have a clearer picture of both events in your own words."

"Okay, Johnny, I guess I should add more to what I briefly covered at the cemetery, although it's still painful after all these years. I guess your mother and I never really fully spoke about those events to you three, much less to the grands and greats. Your mom and I talked about Stevie and Bobby a lot on the bench, but we should have spoken to you three more about it, giving you the facts to pass down to your children and they to their children.

"Stevie didn't survive when a car ran the stop sign at the corner of Pepper and Higuera Streets as he was riding his bike to his first day of school at San Luis Obispo Senior High School. It happened at about seven forty-five a.m. on Monday, September 11, 1961. He was just fourteen years old.

"Ironically, the car was driven by a SLOSH senior, Ted Benson, who was somehow distracted on his way to his first day of classes, also. Toxicology reports indicated that he had not been drinking or taking any drugs, legal or illegal. He pled guilty to involuntary manslaughter and was severely emotionally affected by the incident. At the sentencing phase, Blanchie and I recommended five years of probation, because this was his first brush with the law and because he was an honor student throughout his high school years. We knew he was emotionally destroyed and probably would be for the rest of his life. We figured that this would be a form of life sentence in which he would be imprisoned by guilt and regret.

"Ted and his family moved to Clovis, and he had kept in touch by mail with Blanchie and me over the years. Johnny, Mary, and Timothy, I never told you the details, and, I suppose, we just 'chickened out.' Your mother and I figured why dig up this incident again and the pain it would bring to you and Ted's family."

"Dad, I guess Timothy, Mary, and I have our own little secret, too. Ten years ago we tracked Ted down, who, as you probably know, had lived in Clovis since the accident. As you also must know, I'm sure, he founded a vehicle-driving school with his dad a year after graduating from Clovis High School in 1962, and the school has been very successful nationwide, with fifty locations. Of course, he and his instructors include this incident in each class.

"About five years ago, the three of us met Ted and his wife, Ilene, for the first time. It was a very tearful event that lasted all day at his house,.

"I suppose there was relief on everyone's part during and after this 'better-late-than-never' event, but, boy, were we nervous! Turns out that Ted and Ilene were, too!

"Ted told us that you and Mom had told him several times over the years that you forgave him and that he always wondered if we siblings had forgiven him, too. He said he was too afraid to ask you or to ask you about how to contact us but was so relieved that we had decided to take the initiative.

"Dad, I guess, like you, we didn't want to dredge up unpleasant memories for you and Mom, but it looks like we all did the right thing in the long run, just maybe separately. I hope you are not upset!"

"Johnny, of course I'm not upset! This was always a very sensitive subject, and I guess we all had good intentions behind not telling each other! Now I know why they say that 'confessions are good for the soul'!"

"Dad, Ilene called me three months ago to say that Ted had just passed away from a heart attack. I offered her condolences from Johnny, Mary, and me."

"Thank you, Johnny. Yes, Ilene called me, too, in the same time frame. She never told me that you all knew about Ted and the visit that you had with them. I guess she was being considerate of us all.

"And now I'd like to get back to saying a little about Bobby. You all probably know that Bobby was miscarried on April 26, 1950, at the end of Blanchie's fourth month. The doctor suspected that something was wrong during her routine checkup the day before. He said that the heartbeat was not as strong and regular as it should be and that Mom would have to stay in the hospital for Bobby to be monitored. There was no improvement by the end of the day, and the next morning, April 26, 1950, the doctors did not hear a heartbeat. They monitored Bobby all day, but at six p.m., Mom miscarried our dear little Bobby.

"We have always considered April 26 as Bobby's birthday and entry date into Heaven.

"The losses of Bobby and Stevie really tested our faith. I will admit to times of doubting God's existence, the power of prayer, and so much more. Turns out that Bobby and Stevie's deaths made us more determined to continue our conversations on our bench and to understand these numerous concepts that we discussed on our bench for over seventy years.

"Well, everyone, today has been very taxing on us all. What say we just relax and leave the smartphones and laptops in their cases? I just want to go sit on our bench for a second and feel Mom's presence! I won't be gone long, and when I get back, how 'bout some Scrabble or checkers?"

"Sounds good, Dad. Besides, we all have to get packed for our trips back home tomorrow! Thank you for sharing about Stevie and Bobby; I wanted your grandkids and great-grandkids to hear about them from you! See you in a bit—don't forget to take a sweater!"

seven

Back on the Bench

"My dearest Blanchie, I hope you can hear me. This morning we said good-bye to you, and, as odd as this sounds—did you witness your funeral, just as you did your wake? Both the mass and burial were nice, quick, and simple. I think this was good because we were all emotionally drained; I know I was!

"Anyway, here we are, just you and me, like always, where we did our best thinking and conversing! Oh, how I wish I could see you, hold you, caress you...kiss you!"

"Oh, Bob, yes, I'm right here with you, right now, on our bench! I guess it must be around four p.m., so it seems that we can chat at any time of the day, as long as it's on our bench. How interesting!"

"Yes, honey, this is so comforting, especially now that I need you so!"

"My dearest Bob, I, too, need you so, and I would also love to hold you, caress you, and kiss you! We'll have to wait until you get here...Oh, I do hope you get here. Just kidding, silly Bob!

"How are we able or allowed to have this type of contact when probably no other couple ever has? I don't know, Bob. just like there are still things that I can't answer yet that we discussed over all those years. But I'm doing my best to find out the answers!"

"Blanchie, I suppose this is as good a time as any to tell you. The only secret I ever kept from you all these years was the fact that I often thought about these past few days—you know, when you would no longer be at my side, that is, if you died before me. So many times I wondered what these past days would be like and what my days would be like without you in the future.

"I decided years ago that if you died before me, I would, first, hope to be one of those couples where a spouse died soon after the other. If this didn't happen, I vowed to still 'follow up' on the topics that we most speculated on all these years on my own, those topics dealing with 'Door Number Three, the Afterlife.' Lo and behold, I never dreamed that we would still be conversing—me from Earth and you from Heaven; how unbelievable! I think Johnny, Timothy, and Mary believe that I believe that you and I still converse, but I'm not sure if they really believe it themselves. Can't say that I blame them!

"Okay, Blanchie...so what is behind Door Number Three? Is it anything like we used to talk about? Did you actually enter a door? Are there 'Pearly Gates' with St. Peter at them to greet, or maybe screen, entrants? Was there a white light at any point after you died? What did you see and smell? What did you hear? What did you feel and touch? As Honey Bunches asked, what is the temperature in Heaven? What do you look like? What does everyone look like? Have you seen God the Father, God the Son, and God the Holy Spirit as we were taught in catechism? Are there other gods and heavens according to the different religions...oh, so many things we talked about, and I wanna know everything!"

"Whoa, Bob, hold on; where do I start? Yes, I attended my funeral mass and burial today, as well as my wake last night, never leaving your side on these occasions. I especially cherished everyone who sat next to me all night for their hour-long vigils. Johnny, Timothy, Honey Bunches, and our grands spoke such kind words to me during their hours next to me. I've never felt so close to them, or, for that matter, my dearest Bob, to you, during our hour together. Now, how many times can one say that?"

"Oh, Blanchie, me, too!"

"Before the wake, I thought I would be somewhat scared to listen to some of the comments, but everyone was very kind, loving, and, at times, humorous. I had forgotten that I told the kids about playing Holy Communion with Jimmy Mahoney! My special thanks to you and the kids for your loving words at the wake; I was very moved!"

"Honey, for me, saying a few words to you, and about you, in front of everyone was the hardest thing I had ever done. You know what a crybaby I am! I was so proud of our kids for their kind words and the fact that they got through it without falling apart!"

"I was also very moved that you finally released our little 'secret' about Ted Benson; it was about time that you or I did it! I think it was important that our kids heard it from you, even if they already knew everything from doing their own investigations and contacting Ted and Ilene on their own.

"Well, Bob, it's getting late and I'm tired—yes, we need sleep in Heaven, too, which I'll discuss later! I'll see you tomorrow, seven a.m., right here, okay? I love you so much!"

"I love you too, Blanchie! I'll bring your coffee!"

"Ha, no need, as I make my own! And maybe prepare to say grace for tomorrow morning, too, okay?"

"You got it, honey! Good night!"

eight

Blanchie's Arrival to Heaven

"Good morning, dearest Blanchie. This is day six since you left this earth."

"Good morning, Bob. I'm right here with you again, and I brought my coffee! So, think you could start us off with grace?"

"Okay, honey, here goes one that, again, Father Chuck did not like: as the earthquake hit, the priest told his congregation to leave the church service 'en masse.'"

"Ha, yes, I remember that one and Father Chuck's rather stern reaction! Well, quite a plausible scenario—an earthquake, here in California!"

"Say, Blanchie, I tossed and turned all night! Please, please, tell me about what's behind Door Number Three, you know, the Afterlife, probably the topic we discussed most on this bench!"

"Okay, Bob, well, I'm not even sure where to start. It's all so new to me, so I'm not even sure what's going on. After what I described in the bedroom as I was dying, I saw a light, and it was very soft and comforting. I know that neurologists and other medical experts have often said that this is a physiological reaction of one's body to death. I didn't suffer."

"Oh, honey, I'm so happy that you didn't suffer!"

"Now, Bob, you're gonna think that I've really lost my marbles, but my next memory was of sitting on a chair in our Old Mission's coffee room, where we had coffee and donuts after every Sunday mass! I was surrounded by maybe ten others who, I assume, had just left their earthly existence like me. There was lots of conversational noise—everyone asking questions about where they were and describing their last minutes on Earth. Even though I recognized three people that I know only spoke Spanish, I heard bits and pieces of their conversation in English. It seems that everyone in Heaven hears foreign languages in their native tongue, just as we had speculated.

"Bob, you'll never guess where I'm told I'll be for five hours a day, starting in two days—at this very same coffee room and adjacent classrooms, just four blocks from our house and two blocks away from our bench! Some kind of weeklong orientation classes of a sort!

"You guessed it, Bob; I don't think that I've even left SLO! Well, I mean, I'm here in what I'm told is a parallel universe!"

"Oh, Blanchie, I knew it! How many times did we speculate that Heaven is a parallel universe, that we continued to live on Earth in some kind of 'other' dimension, maybe even in our hometown?"

"Bob, remember the saying 'Heaven on Earth'? Well, Heaven *is* Earth! Oh, there's so much I don't know, but I promise I'm doing my best to find out! Now, remember how we often asked ourselves 'what is our purpose on Earth,' and 'why is Earth so temporary?' From what I can gather, it seems that we all are on Earth to prepare ourselves for Heaven!

"And, Bob, hold on tight to the bench—I'll be going home every afternoon after my classes! That's right, the home that we shared for seventy-one years! How wonderful and weird is that? In fact, I've been sleeping in our bed since I died! Oh, Bob, that lump that was forever on my side—no longer there!"

"Oh, Blanchie, this is unbelievable news! I can't believe what is happening!"

"Neither can I, Bob! Okay, back to the Old Mission's coffee room. It and the adjacent offices and rooms have been remodeled to act as a reception site with maybe three classrooms, as well as bedrooms for those who need them—each with an individual-size bed, a bathroom, closet space, computer with Internet access, and one of those newfangled, what are they called, plasma flat-screen TVs. If a married couple arrives at the same time, which is very rare, they are assigned a larger room with a large bed. There is a shared laundry facility down the hall. Yes, we still have to do laundry in Heaven!"

"So, Blanchie, I hope that people 'air their dirty laundry' less in Heaven!"

"That's right, silly Bob, king of the one-liners! Speaking of so-called jokes, I want to find out if there is humor in Heaven, as we had discussed on our bench! I'm sure there is, as everything up to now seems identical to Earth.

"Anyway, back on track. I'm not sure yet, but it appears that each city or town throughout the world has similar reception sites, places in Heaven where persons of specific faiths, like Catholics, Protestants, Muslims, Jews, Buddhists, Hindus, etc., first arrive after leaving Earth. Some of the staff here have told me that, wherever the reception site, this is where the person attends some kind of orientation in which they are introduced to Heaven from the perspective of their specific religion and town—in my case, from a Catholic perspective.

"You and I had speculated for years about the concept of other religions having their own heavens, and the answer seems to be no, that, in Heaven, everyone is part of this parallel universe just as they were on Earth.

"Oh, Bob, I know I'm bouncing around. I'm just so excited, and all of this is so new!

"Before, you asked about the 'Pearly Gates' and St. Peter! I saw nothing of either one. I'll have to follow up on these notions and see if they exist now or ever did. I strongly suspect that these were just ideas or visions of Heaven, much like the elaborate paintings of cherubims that I'm told don't exist.

"This orientation period lasts about a week, so I'll be asking a lot of questions! These classes start in two days for me."

"Oh, Blanchie, I'm so excited! Please, please, ask a million questions inside and outside of your classes with the staff and our neighbors!"

"Of course—did you really think you had to ask me? Have I ever not been curious or at a loss for words?"

"Good point, Miss Blanchie!"

"Bob, I think it would be a good idea for both of us not to tell anyone anything about our secret communication. For some reason, I think that I've been chosen to reveal information about the afterlife to you and only you. I don't know why, because everyone still living would like to know all this stuff, right? Remember how many times we wondered why we never hear from or about the deceased, except in brief encounters between mediums and one's relatives—you know, the ones we used to see on the History Channel? I'll talk about that later when I have more information, as it will be included in a future class.

"If for no other reason, let's make it our secret so as not to jinx it and cause someone to take it away from us! Besides, you don't want to see the inside of the loony bin!

"Oh Bob, when you and Mary get to Heaven, you'll find out that the temperature in Heaven is exactly the same as on Earth, as, again, Heaven appears to be a parallel universe to Earth. In other words, it is the same Earth we all know or knew! Many scientists and religious scholars have often speculated on this idea of a parallel universe, and it seems to be true! Remember how the Bible says that man was made in the image and likeness of God? It's a similar concept that Heaven is a mirror image of Earth!"

"Honey, remember how we speculated about whether there are humans just like us on other planets? Recently we also saw news reports about this, too. This would really throw the proverbial monkey wrench into all these issues! And, speaking of planets, we occasionally talked about the planets that astronomers were constantly discovering in the vast expanses of the universe and how impacting it would be if life—especially human life—were to be found on them!"

"Yes, Bob, and this is an issue that I want to get to the bottom of!

"Okay, getting back on track, remember the movie with Sandra Bullock and Keanu Reeves, *The Lake House*? Everyone in Heaven appears to be sharing Earth with all of you 'living folk' at the same time, as opposed to the two-year time lag in communication between these two actors in the movie. I'm still trying to figure out why or how you and I can communicate in, as they say, 'real time.' Even though you can't see or touch me, you 'hear' me as my voice in your brain. I'm hesitant to ask about all this, as no one seems to know that you and I are having these chats, but I'll keep you updated when I get answers, even if those answers are 'I don't know!'

"Bob, there are other issues related to this concept of a parallel universe, but I want to address them later. Let's try to discuss and describe more fundamental things first, as well as things that I have answers to—few as they might be. Keep in mind that I just don't know a lot of things at this early stage, and I have not been able to ask many of our long-standing questions yet. Rest assured that I will, during this orientation period and beyond."

"Blanchie, what do you and everyone else look like? Remember this was a topic we discussed a lot!"

"Bob, from what one of the staff members has told me, everyone appears to be at different ages, depending on who they're talking to. It's hard to understand, much less explain, but I do have an example: Yesterday I saw my high school classmate, Karen Vanlerbergh, whom I hadn't seen since high school graduation in 1938. She's one of the staff assisting with orientation and came to Heaven four years ago. To me, she looks to be seventeen years old, like the last time I saw her. She said that I look seventeen, too. I have no earthly—I mean, heavenly—idea of how or why this is!

"Everyone seems to have the same body that they had on Earth. I know this is true for me! I'm told that a possible exception to this observation is a fetus. Karen said that if the fetus dies through abortion or a miscarriage, they arrive here to this reception area in a thirty-year-old body, speaking and hearing what his or her native language would have been. I hope to find out more about this whole age topic!

"Bob, I know I'm sort of jumping around, but you and I used to talk about the existence of Purgatory, Limbo, and Hell. So far, I've just heard the scuttlebutt of those around me, but I'm told that, of the three, only Hell exists. These were always very important topics, and I will address them later as I get more answers in my classes."

"Blanchie, I can't express how perfectly odd this all sounds and feels! You left this earth only to stay in the same California town that you and I grew up in and where we both lived our whole lives! The fact that somehow we are able to hear each other—you in Heaven and me on Earth—is the strangest part of all!"

"Oh, Bob, I agree with you one hundred percent, and I'm doing my best to make sense of all this!

"Well, let me describe a little more of what I've been going through! I think that this is my fourth day in Heaven, and I am very, very happy! My 'arrival' to this reception area consisted of suddenly finding myself here at the Old Mission's coffee hall, standing in line to, I guess you could say, 'check into' Heaven, much like checking into a hotel! As I mentioned, I'd say there are about ten of us here, everyone full of questions, but mostly jubilation; after all, we have all just won the lottery!

"I'm told that everyone who goes to Heaven arrives at this same type of reception station that is run by their own local church in their own community."

"Honey, this is an adventure that we'll both go through together! I'm excited about maybe learning more and lessening some of the mystery surrounding the topics that we discussed for so many years, so keep asking questions!"

"Some of the initial things I noticed are that everyone feels pain, hunger, and goes to the bathroom, just as we did on Earth! Just ask my knee that I hit on our coffee table many times at home—you know, the 'dag-blasted coffee table' that you had so many encounters with over the years! I'm told that we can get injured, just as on Earth, but that no one can die! I hope to have more to say about this as orientation progresses!

"Okay, Bob, there'll be plenty more to talk about tomorrow! I must be getting to my classes! I'll talk to you tomorrow, okay? I love you so much!"

"Okay, Blanchie. I love you too! Tomorrow, if I could, I'd like to mention some of the topics we covered over the years, just as a reminder of what answers to look out for!"

"Okay, Bob, sounds good, but you won't have to remind me of many. We'll talk tomorrow!"

nine

Message from the Kids

"Okay, Blanchie, but hold up a second before you go to class. The kids and the entire brood are coming toward our bench. I'm sure they want to say good-bye before heading back home. Honey, the kids don't know about our conversations; I say we keep it that way."

"That's fine, Bob. I agree. Maybe later we can tell the kids."

"Hi, kids, come on over! Well, I feel Mom and Grandma Blanchie's presence on our bench. I know this sounds crazy. Come on; come and say hi to her!"

The entire family surrounds Bob and the bench. They seem somewhat hesitant to greet their deceased mother, grandmother, and great grandmother, but they know that it's important to Bob that they do.

"Hi, Mom. This is Tim. I'm here with Dad, Mary, Johnny, and all your grands and greats! We have to get going now, but we feel your presence here and wherever we go. All of us live only one-to-three hours away, and we've discussed with Dad coming up with a schedule for each of us to spend one weekend a month helping him out around the house and keeping him company. As always, we'll continue to call him three times a week! Mom, we all love you so much! What do we say here… talk to you later? Everyone, say good-bye to Grandpa Bob and Grandma Blanchie!"

"Oh, how I love all of my grands and greats! Now, you tell me if your parents and grandparents don't spoil you enough, and I will!"

"Kids, Grandpa Bob was just kidding; weren't you, Dad? Mom, this is Honey Bunches. Your husband in incorrigible! I'm sure that Heaven is wonderful, and hopefully I'll find out about the temperature then, right? I love you and miss you, and, like Timothy said, we'll all continue to take care of Dad and keep him company!"

"Hey, Mom, this is Johnny! Not much I can add except to say how much I love you and to thank you for being the best mom and grandma ever! As Father Chuck said, you will definitely be inducted into the 'Mother Hall of Fame' in the first round! I love you and will continue to ask you for your advice! As Timothy and Mary said, we, too, will continue to take care of Dad from Fresno! And yes, we'll all drive carefully back home. I know you are saying that as we speak!"

"Johnny, that's my line, too! Everyone, please drive careful!"

"Bob, when the kids leave, I want to talk to you again!"

"Dad, can we walk you to the house?"

"No, thanks, Johnny, I think I'll stay here and keep talking to your Mom! I'll be okay. Please drive carefully and call me when you get home! Even though you're receiving Social Security, you're still my babies, and I'll always be concerned for your safety!"

One by one, Timothy, Mary, Johnny, and all the grands and greats kissed Bob on the forehead and started for the house, while he stayed on the bench to continue talking to Blanchie. Bob waited until he couldn't see them anymore, and then he broke down. Everything just hit him at that very instant, especially the fact that he was going to be alone—well, except from 7:00 to 8:00 a.m. when he had his Blanchie all to himself!

"Oh, Bob, please don't cry; now you're making me cry, too! You'll still see the kids, grands, and greats a lot, like always, maybe just not all at the same time as over the last few days! They are the main reason that we have maintained a healthy and youthful outlook on life."

"Honey, you're righter than rain!"

"By the way, Bob, I keep mentioning our bench because it seems that we only have this special, direct communication while we're sitting on it! I don't want to ask why, for fear that this privilege will be taken away! I guess if you want to talk to me at another time of the day, go to our bench, which appears to be the key, as it seems that I cannot see, touch, or talk to you anywhere else. Our daily seven-to-eight time slot seems to be best, as my orientation classes last from nine a.m. to three p.m. Monday through Friday, but maybe we could try after three p.m. from our bench, just to see if it works, okay?

"Hey, did I mention that I sleep in our bed every night? Yeah, I think I told you that the nasty lump on my side is gone! How weird is that?"

"Oh, honey, this is all such a blur and so surreal! Can I say 'sleep tight and don't let the bedbugs bite'? Wait, uh, I guess there are no bedbugs in Heaven, right?"

"No, that's not true, Bob! Remember that this is a parallel universe, which means that there are bedbugs, cucarachas, ants, flies, and mosquitos, too! Speaking of bugs, I wonder if Mr. Andre is still the owner of Bugs Begone here in Heaven, too! I'll have to go see him to say hi. I think his house was on Marsh and Pismo Streets, across the street from Foster's Freeze, which, by the way, is still there.

"Okay, Bob, I'll talk to you tomorrow morning, okay? I'm anxious to start my classes and continue asking so many questions. I love you so much!"

"I love you too, Honey. What say, tomorrow, you and I start our new life together, our own 'afterlife'!"

"Oh, Bob, you put it so sweet. Yes, let's do!"

ten

Bob Meets Two Very Special Persons

"Good morning, Blanchie. Are you here with me on the bench? I know today is your first day of classes! It's seven a.m. here. What time is it in Heaven, and what time zone are you in? This is kind of a special day, as it's our first day alone together, back on our bench!"

"Good morning, Bob; yes, I'm right here next to you. Howzabout grace before we start?"

"Okay, honey. The girl loved to ride horses but didn't want to be saddled with preparing them to ride."

"Yes, Bob, nor did she want to stirrup trouble! Remember when I used to finish that pun like that? See? You're not the only one who can tell a bad joke!

"Let me first say that I love you and that I am in the same time zone as you! Remember, we are both in SLO! Yes, today is very special because it's our first morning alone since I arrived to Heaven. But it's also special for two other reasons that you're not going to believe! Hang on to the bench, Bob!"

"Oh, Blanchie, I love you too! Say, uh, honey, I, uh, well, uh, I was wondering, well…"

"Say no more, Bob. I know what you're going to ask! Yes, Bobby Jr. is right here with me! Bob, did you hear me?"

"Oh, Blanchie, yes, I'm here; I just can't believe this is happening! Can I…can I talk with him? Can he talk? How old is he?"

"Silly Bob, why don't you ask Bobby yourself? I'm on your right, and Bobby is seated immediately to your left! He can hear and see you, but you can only hear him in your mind, like with me! Seems that those of us in Heaven can see and hear you, but you can only hear us! I don't know why! Bob…Bob?"

"Hello, Daddy!"

"Son, er, Bobby, I don't quite know what to call you! Oh, my God, is this really happening? I've never met you except to feel you move inside Mommy. I love you so much! Not one day has passed that I haven't told you and Mommy this! Oh, Bobby, I hope you don't mind me calling you that and referring to your mother as 'Mommy.' This is my first time meeting you, just as if you were a newborn, and this is how I would talk to you!"

"Daddy, I don't mind at all! I suppose that, at some point, I'll call each of you Mom and Dad, but until then, Mommy and Daddy sound pretty good! Yes, as Mommy said, I can see and hear you for the first time! I had only seen photos of you. This is so, so strange but happy!"

"And I can hear you, too, son; I just can't see or touch you! You have a good, strong voice!"

"Thanks, Daddy. Mommy and I stayed up all night at your—well, our—house! She says that I shouldn't say anything about these conversations to anyone here in Heaven, so I won't!

"Daddy, I chose to be twenty-seven years old, even though I died at six months inside Mommy's womb in 1949! You see, at any time, anyone in Heaven can choose whatever age they want to be, but most see others at the age they knew them most! How this works, I really don't know.

"Daddy, there are so many cases like mine—children either aborted on purpose or by Mother Nature, like me! Consequently, yes, as you and Mommy discussed for so many years on your bench, there is usually some kind of reunion between son or daughter and the parents in Heaven at some point. This might be hard to believe, but in the case of an intentional abortion, there rarely are bad feelings on the part of the aborted offspring or their parents toward them, as Heaven is mostly absent of bad feelings and full of forgiveness and understanding! In most miscarriages, parents meet their aborted offspring and build relationships with them, just like with Mommy and me, and, and by the way, like with my grandparents and me—obviously before Mommy got to Heaven.

"As you can see, I've been rather 'tuned in' to the whole subject of abortion and have met a lot of parents and aborted children since arriving to Heaven. In the case of conception as a result of rape, whether or not the child is aborted, miscarried, or allowed to be born, the biological mothers and offspring in Heaven often meet and begin a 'better-late-than-never' relationship. Unfortunately, as on Earth, fathers in rape cases seem to be less likely to want a relationship with the child or the mother. Oftentimes, the father does not go to Heaven, but even from Hell, the fathers do not request to see their children or the mothers. I don't know how often reunions happen in these circumstance, nor how they are carried out.

"This whole issue serves to emphasize the importance of being responsible on Earth, as most of one's actions on Earth carry over into Heaven in one form or another!

"Daddy, Mommy will fill you in on my life, between her miscarriage and the time she joined me here in Heaven just a few days ago. By the way, I've lived in our—your—old house since arriving to Heaven in 1949! The house is doing great, and I've started making memories with Mommy. When you, Johnny, Timothy, Mary, and everyone else get here, we'll make new ones!"

"Oh, Bobby, I can hardly wait! I so wish I could see you!"

"Well, Daddy, Mommy says I look like your clone! I don't think that's a compliment. Just kidding!

"Daddy, please, please say hi to Timothy, Mary, Johnny, and their families! Please tell them that I love them and have thought of them every day here in Heaven! Daddy, I love you so!

"Oh, by the way, Daddy, Mommy has another surprise for you. Mom, if you don't mind, I'm going to spill the beans, okay? Dad, Mommy said there were two reasons that today is very special!"

"Oh, no, Bobby, I just can't take it. Don't tell me. Please make it be true…"

"Dad? Dad, I'm right here, and you look great! Dad? Dad? Oh, Dad, please don't cry! This is Stevie…Dad? I'm looking right at you, and yes, I'm crying too! Mommy and Bobby also—we're all crying!"

"Stevie, my dear, dear Stevie! I'm crying for joy and because I'm overwhelmed at this moment after speaking with Bobby for the first time ever…and now you! Oh, how I've missed you so! Why, why were you taken from Mommy and me at age fourteen? You were riding your bike at the corner of Pepper and Higuera, such an ordinary intersection. It was to be your first day at San Luis Senior High School!

"Son, I just can't believe I'm talking to you! I have so many questions!"

"Yes, Dad, I'm sure we'll be talking a lot before and after you come to Heaven. Hey, whooda thunk that Heaven would be San Luis Obispo? Remember the old Chamber of Commerce slogan on all the highway billboards: 'SLO…Go! It's a Piece of Heaven!'

"Oh, Dad, I love you so much! Mommy says we'll be able to talk often as long as you're on the bench! There are so many questions I have, too! And, like Bobby said, please, please give my love to Johnny, Timothy, Mary, and their families and to all my nieces, nephews, and great-nieces and-nephews!

"Dad, I'll talk to you later, I guess! I love you so much!"

"Oh, sons, I love you both so much, too! Yes, we'll talk later and very often! We have so much to catch up on and Bobby, especially in your case, to discover! You two enjoy Mommy, okay, and help her out with the housecleaning and taking care of the yard! By the way, Johnny, Mary, and Timothy sent their love to you through Mommy many times at the wake, both masses, and at the internment. Also, so you know, over the years, they have always talked about you and remembered you with love."

"Well, Bob…Talk about two once-in-a-lifetime surprises! You had to know they were coming! Bobby and Stevie are so handsome, and we're making up for lost time. They keep reminding me, 'Mommy, we have forever!' On Earth, that was an expression; here it's a reality!

"Bob, I have to get going to my class. I love you so much, and we'll talk tomorrow, okay?"

"Okay, sure, Blanchie. I think I'll need the time to recover! This has been one of the happiest days of my life; thank you! I, too, love you so much!"

"And for me, too, honey. We'll talk in the morning!"

eleven

Blanchie's Parents

"Good morning, Blanchie. I'm here on our bench! This is our second day alone, but somehow I don't feel so lonely, knowing that you are here with me! I love you so!"

"Good morning, Bob. Yes, I am right here, and I love you too! My classes are going well. I'll let you know bits and pieces. Oh, Bob, I have the best news!

"Last night Mommy and Daddy came to visit me at our house! We hugged and cried for what seemed to be forever before we sat in the living room and talked until two a.m.! I'm still running on adrenaline, but, Bob, here's the best news: they're right here with me on the bench, and they still live in the same house that I grew up in! They can see and hear you, and they send you their love! Hold on, and I'll let you chat!"

"Hi, Bob. This is Sallie! We are fine and very happy here in Heaven! You look great! I simply can't believe how all of us can communicate with you on the bench! You are the only person on Earth who is getting information directly from Heaven while you're still on Earth. Whoops, Blanche told me not to say that. Well, what are they gonna do, send me to Hell or back to Earth?

"Chuck and I told you many times on Earth, and we'll tell you again how lucky Blanche and our grandkids, great-grandkids, and great-great-grandkids are, and were, to have you in their lives! Bob, you are one of the best wood engraver artisans in the world, and you have always focused on what you were most passionate about—wood engraving. You were not as successful financially as your work merited, but you were a super

46

husband and parent, always putting Blanche and your family first! This is what is most important in life!

"We love you and are anxious to get news from Earth from you through Blanche, and, yes, we know not to say anything about any of this!

"By the way, Bob, we've been seeing Bob Jr. and Stevie two or three times a week since we arrived to Heaven! What handsome men they are, although I think they got their good looks from Blanche! Oh, c'mon, Bob; you know I'm just kidding! We hope to talk to you soon!"

"Oh, Sallie and Chuck, what a thrill to talk to you! Can you believe it? I love you too and will certainly keep you informed on the goings-on back here at home! I hope we can talk often!"

"Mommy, Daddy, if you don't mind, I need to get to class! Bob, how about we talk tomorrow at seven?"

"Okay, Blanchie, and thank you so much for arranging this visit with your parents. I love you!"

"I love you, too, Bob! Let's see what other surprises I can come up with for tomorrow!"

twelve

Speeder and Grammie Poke

"Blanchie, I really enjoyed hearing from your parents yesterday! Well, I guess on a similar subject, I was wondering, maybe, have you, do you…?"

"Yes, Bob, I also have great news today, too! Last night I had a long visit with your mother! It was so great to see her, the first time I'd seen her since I arrived in Heaven. We talked until six this morning, and guess what? Well, guess what, silly Bob?"

"Oh, Blanchie, please don't tell me…it can't be…I mean…"

"Yes, Bob, your mom is right here! We just came from the house and haven't slept at all! Here she is!"

"Oh, Bobby, is this really you? It's me, Speeder!"

"Yes, Speeder, it's me! Are you really next to me on the bench?"

"Yes, Bobby, I am on your right, and I can hear and see you! This is so very odd! I never imagined we'd have any type of contact before we met in Heaven! I miss you, and I love you!

"I've had weekly contact with Bobby, Stevie, and Blanche's parents over the years, and we have become very close in Heaven.

"Bob, I've thought of you every day since I died in 1972. There's a kind of Facebook system here in Heaven that lets us know what relatives and friends have died and what's going on with our kids and grandkids, like graduations, weddings, major successes, etc. I'm so proud of Johnny, Timothy, Mary, and all of your extended family! You all have been successful in life and have raised wonderful families from generation to generation!

"My life in Heaven has been pretty much the same life that I had on Earth toward the end of my life: working in the yard of our green

Chinese house, visiting my best friends Moira, Richard, Jean, and Anita, and watching HNN—Heaven News Network. You know, Bob, we get these news channels here in Heaven, but they only show good news and happy, optimistic news from Heaven, not from Earth. Sure, everyone knows that there are ugly things happening on Earth, and we can see them on mainstream Earth news channels if we really want, but most prefer not to. I still don't know how all this works!

"Bob, I know what your next question is, and yes, Dad is here in Heaven! We've long since made amends—well, I guess he has long since made amends with me. He admitted his severe emotional abuse of me and you, along with the effect this had on you as you grew up. Dad lives here in town, and we see each other maybe once a month since I came to Heaven. You'll remember that Dad died six years before me, in 1966. If you wish, I can arrange a visit between you two. Long ago he said that he'd like to talk to you, and now it looks like you two, if you want, would be able to talk in this forum!"

"Well, Speeder, I just don't know. We'll see."

"Oh, Bob, Stevie and Bobby have a great relationship with Dad! You won't recognize him; he's loving, attentive, funny, and generous with his time and advice. Also, if you'd like, I can talk to Blanchie about arranging a visit for you and me with Dad's parents and family members in Illinois. I, like you, had never met them here on Earth, but we've visited I guess ten times over the years. They're such nice people!"

"But you, Speeder, you say you've made amends with Dad? Are you sure?"

"Yes, Bob, remember that here in Heaven, there are very few bad feelings. Don't ask me how, but that's how things are! Family feuds and feuds between friends no longer exist in Heaven!

"Okay, Bob, brace yourself again! Guess who else is here right now? Grammie Poke!"

"Oh, my God, Speeder, is this really true? Grammie Poke? Are you here next to me? Oh, Grammie, how I love you!"

"Bobby...Bobby? This is Grammie Poke! Oh, Bobby, I haven't seen you since you were twenty, when I came here to Heaven! I, too, love and miss you and have been so proud of your life's accomplishments over the years! I live in the same green Chinese-style house on Palm Street, along with your mom, Bobby Jr, Stevie, and my parents! I know you did so many repairs to it over the years, but the house is in perfect condition here in Heaven!

"Oh, and Bobby Jr. and Stevie are such sweet men and look just like you! Did Sallie say they looked just like Blanchie?

"Bobby, you've probably wondered about your grandfather, Carl Fisher, all these years. I told your mother last night and suppose I should let her talk to you about him, but I'll steal some of her thunder! Bob, over the years on Earth, I never spoke to you or your mom about him— why and how he disappeared when your mom was just two years old. I didn't speak about him because I didn't know much about his past or what had actually happened to him, and I also didn't know if I should be embarrassed or not, as in those days, this type of situation was pretty much hush-hush!

"Well, Bobby, he's here in Heaven and lives in Germany, where he was born and raised. He looked me up when I arrived to Heaven, and he spent a week here with us, explaining what had happened.

"Oh, Bobby, Carl and I met and quickly married in SLO in July of 1899. Claire, or Speeder, as you call your mother, was born in Los Angeles on April 26, 1900, because Carl was assigned down there to a private cargo vessel firm, and that's where we lived and where we were going to live. In May of 1902, he accepted a well-paying job to sail to South America and back, a trip that was to take eighteen months. I declined to go because your mom was just two years old, and the trip would have been very hard on her and me.

"It seems that Carl's ship sunk off the coast of Chile in very rough seas seven months later. His family in Germany was notified because his information was found washed ashore. My information was never found, and his family didn't know about me, and, therefore, didn't know how to contact me. Your mother and I have since gone several times to Germany to visit Carl and his family. They are wonderful people and want to add you and your family to theirs! I haven't had a chance to contact him about Blanche. But I will, so we can all have a nice chat!

"Oh, Bob, Carl is so nice, and we have had such great visits over the years! We have weekly contact, usually by phone, and he visits once a year. He deeply regrets how things turned out, but is very, very proud of your mother, and how her family has turned out. She and Carl have monthly contact and your mother so wants you to meet him, too!

"I've caught him up on everything that has happened on your mother's side of the family. I'm sure he'll be just thrilled to talk with you and, someday, with Johnny, Timothy, and Mary! He already has monthly contact with Bobby Jr and Stevie, and they have been to Germany to meet his family!

"Oh, Bobby, I love you so much, and I have missed you over all these years!"

"Me, too, Grammie Poke! I remember you very well, and Mom talked about you every day after you passed! One thing I remember maybe most about you was how you ate cereal with orange juice and a persimmon at your kitchen table! Mom says you were allergic to milk. Ha! I always admired you for being a single mother, which in your day was much harder and had a stigma attached to it, although I never noticed it. You were totally dedicated to Mom and me. In my teens, I learned that you paid for our dental bills and grammar school tuition and I'm sure much, much more!

"Oh, and Grammie Poke, don't think I have forgotten how you used to cook our Thanksgiving dinner after donning a pair of men's underwear on your head!"

"Oh my gosh, Bobby, did you really remember that? I started wearing them when everyone was asleep in the morning, but I always forgot to take them off! And, no, don't ask me where I got them. I think they belonged to my grandpa John!"

"Grammie Poke, I hope you and I can talk often! I'm anxious to learn more about my great-grandpa John and my great-uncle Timothy and to maybe even talk to them! You know that I named two of my boys after them and Mary after you! I so want to tell you about my life and learn about yours, both on Earth and in Heaven! There are so many questions I still have about your childhood! Listen, Grammie, I'm no spring chicken, so you and I will probably see each other sooner than later. Well, that is, of course, well—you know!

"I love you, Grammie Poke and you, too, Speeder! I'll talk to both of you soon!"

"Bob, I should get ready to go to my orientation classes. Remember not to tell anyone about these encounters, okay? I've told our family members here that mum's the word! I'll be here on the bench tomorrow at seven a.m. with bells on! I love you so much!"

"Oh, Blanchie, thank you so, so much for arranging these precious meetings! I'm on cloud nine! I'll talk to you in the morning! I love you too!"

thirteen

God

At this point, our story makes a logical transition from not being as oriented on Bob, Blanchie, and their family but now beginning to focus on the questions and issues to which they dedicated each morning for seventy-one years on their park bench. This next phase naturally turns to the possibility that Blanchie, being in Heaven, just might be able to answer some of these all-important questions and issues, or at least begin to do so.

"Good morning, Bob. First, I love you! I'm right next to you with my favorite mug—you know, the one you bought me at Dodger Stadium in 1974! I was so scared over the years to drop it, but here it is!"

"Good morning, Blanchie. I love you too! Yes, I remember buying you that 'blasted coffee mug' at Dodger Stadium, and do you know why I remember?"

"Bob, just how could I not remember, as many times as you reminded me? I sent you to the center field concessions area right under the bleachers to get me that coffee mug that I had always wanted. You must have heard the crowd go crazy when Steve Garvey hit a home run that landed in the bullpen, just inches from where you had been sitting on the end of the row before I sent you! You never stopped reminding me of how you would have caught the ball had I not sent you for 'that blasted coffee mug'!"

"Honey, I'm really sorry; truth is, when it comes right down to it, I'm sure I would never have caught the ball bare-handed or even with my baseball glove that I had left at home! I always loved 'that blasted coffee

53

mug'; it was a part of us and sat with us on our bench for over thirty-five years, more than making up for its outrageous price of three dollars!

"Say, Blanchie, why do you let us get so off track?"

"You're right, Bob, it's all my fault; why don't you start us off with grace?"

"Well, I guess we kinda have gotten off track these past few days; I don't think either you or I was quite in the mood for 'grace,' but maybe now we are! Okay, here goes: Detroit's car industry turned out quite a 'bumper crop' last year! Pa-doom bom."

"Yes, Bob, of course I remember that one—a classic for sure!"

"Honey, now that the hoopla has more or less quieted down, I'm dying, so to speak, to touch more directly on the issues that we discussed over the years. What say you? Even though you know most of these topics, I'd like to mention some of them, if you don't mind, at least to refresh your memory. Maybe you could tell me what, if anything, you've heard about them in the short time you've been in Heaven!"

"That's fine, Bob. I very much want to see if I can find out the answers to these topics we discussed for so many years. At least now, at the beginning of my arrival to Heaven, I might not know, but believe me, Bob, I'll never stop trying to get the answers! Our weeklong orientation is a series of classes on many, but not most, of these topics as given, of course, from the Catholic perspective. I'm guessing that I'm not going to get a lot of answers, as these questions are going to be too controversial, just as they are on Earth. I'm hoping that the classes will touch on the Protestant points of view, too. After all, Catholics and Protestants are all Christians and, in my humble opinion, should really be lumped together in the same classes.

"By the way, Bob, you and I always used 'Protestant' and 'Christian' **interchangeably.** I'm told that they are essentially the same term, with slight differences, but maybe we could still use them interchangeably?"

"Sounds good to me, honey!"

"I'm also hoping that, in some way, these classes will cover non-Christian points of view on these same topics—you know, like from Muslims, Jews, Hindus, etc. Needless to say, these should be interesting classes, but I think that I'm going to learn more by talking to people of all faiths outside of them. Funny, I always thought that when I arrived to Heaven, I would know everything!"

"Well, honey, I look forward to having at least some of our topics—should I say, demystified, if not now, then in the future as you continue to do your heavenly detective work! Here are at least some of the topics as I recall them, I guess in no particular order, which I hope will serve as a reminder in your investigations.

"How about we start off with all of our questions about God?"

"Bob, say no more. I know them all by heart, but I'm going to disappoint you because I have no answers yet. But here goes...

"Maybe the biggest 'God question' that we never figured out was: is there more than one god, like one per Catholics, Muslims, Jews, etc.? Another question for us was always: If there is more than one god, using the creationist theory, which one or ones created the universe, including Earth, Heaven, and Hell? Or, in the case of the evolution theory, which gods have been in place over these fourteen billion or so years, and what role, if any, have they had in the evolution of the Earth, Heaven, and Hell? I know these questions almost sound blasphemous to even contemplate, but, Bob, as soon as I find out, I'll let you know!

"Who are God the Father, God the Son, and God the Holy Spirit, the three entities that make up the Holy Trinity? Does the Holy Trinity exist in one person, one god? If so, are they real people? How many Protestant religions believe in the Holy Trinity? To which of the three do we refer to as God—is it God the Father, as we were taught in catechism? Has God always existed, and will He always exist? How could this be? Maybe there is no god; maybe everything happens according to nature's random plan, as we discussed in the theory of evolution?

"Besides serving Catholics, do God the Father, God the Son, and God the Holy Spirit in some way or ways serve all Christians and all people in the world, regardless of their religious denominations or lack thereof?"

"Blanchie, you do remember all of our topics! We should have written a book but not told Father Chuck!"

"You're so right, Bob; such a book would have sent Father Chuck directly to Heaven!

"Remember how many hours and years we spent in our own adult Bible and catechism classes discussing the Holy Trinity, then teaching it in our kids' classes, and then discussing it on our bench? Well, this concept is still not clear yet to me or my classmates here at orientation. On Earth, we believed in the physical existence of God the Father and God the Son, Jesus, but it was never clear about God the Holy Spirit. To make matters more confusing, God the Holy Spirit was always portrayed as a white dove. You and I always thought that God the Holy Spirit was not a real person, per se, but rather a gift from God the Father or God the Son; this was never clear. So, yes, you and I were always very confused. Answering these questions about the Trinity is so very important to me!

"Say, Bob, speaking of the Holy Trinity, remember when our Mary was, I guess, about six years old, and I think one of the topics at the previous Sunday school class had been the Holy Trinity? You and I were in the kitchen and she asked us, 'How can there be three bodies in one? Doesn't it get kinda crowded?' I remember you were on the other side of the kitchen and quickly exited to the living room because you were probably splitting a gut laughing so hard! Mary was so cute and insightful at such an early age!"

"Yes, I remember that famous 'kitchen incident'! I've always wondered how you managed to keep a straight face in front of Honey Bunches! And you're right; I did run out of the kitchen trying to muffle my laughter!"

"Okay, Bob, putting aside the Holy Trinity concept and just referring to 'God,' we were always taught that He is all knowing. With this in mind, how could people be born that He must have known would end up doing atrocious things and eventually going to Hell?"

"I know, Blanchie, like so many murderers, mass murderers and dictators."

"I so very much want to find out this answer!"

"I haven't met, much less seen photos or videos of, the Holy Trinity, nor the Virgin Mary, but I will continue to investigate! In orientation, there doesn't seem to be a slot when we meet them or see their real images, as in at least a prerecorded welcome video. But, as always, I'm on it! Oh, Bob, these issues will maybe be the tallest order!

I think that answering them, if this is possible, will take collaboration with many other religions and will be a part of that detective work you mentioned!"

"Say, Blanchie, dear, you don't seem to need any prompting from me, not after seventy-one years!"

"Oh, Bob, all these topics were the center of our life together every morning, discussing them on our bench for seventy-one years!"

fourteen

Who Is Mary?

"Honey, a good follow-up to our God discussion just now is probably Mary, whom we discussed and speculated on so many times over the years! I'm sure the subject of her has come up in your classes. As Catholics, you and I grew up calling her the Blessed Virgin Mary, the Earthly Mother of Jesus, and we were taught that she conceived him as a virgin through the Immaculate Conception.

"I guess my first questions about Mary are somewhat unrelated but are ones that you and I discussed so many times! We never found the Immaculate Conception phenomenon as mysterious as to how he, God the Father, and God the Holy Spirit have always existed, which presupposes that they were never born or created at any earlier point. The term 'God the Son' also presupposes that Jesus somehow is biologically related to God the Father, not to Mary. So many questions, Blanchie!

"Our dear Mexican friends, José Antonio and Martita, revered Mary, as most Mexicans and Catholics worldwide do. She is considered the patron saint of Mexico, having appeared to the peasant Juan Diego in 1531 in what is now Mexico City, where today the Basilica of Guadalupe is located in her honor. So, Blanchie, what have you learned or heard about Mary—including about her personal life, where she grew up, her parents, etc.?"

"Oh, Bob, I'm going to disappoint you and me again. As with the subject of God, I have not heard anything about Mary that you and I weren't taught on Earth. In our classes, we learned that only the Christian and Muslim faiths believed that Mary was the earthly, biological mother of Jesus, that the Muslims believe that she was not a virgin, and that Jesus was one of twenty-five prophets.

"In our classes, we've touched on the subject of Mary, but we haven't learned anything new. And I see nothing planned to meet her in person or through any kind of video presentation, either.

"I would give anything to meet her and ask her so many questions, especially about her role as the mother of Jesus and her all-too-infrequent appearances worldwide over the years to various humble people. I'd like to ask her why there is so little information about, and contact with her, God the Father, God the Son, God the Holy Spirit, and the saints. Remember how we theorized about who Mary, the human being, was, and what the years were like as Jesus grew up with her and his earthly father, Joseph? As a mother myself, the subject of Mary is very dear to my heart. And I'm determined to find out more and report back to you."

fifteen

Creation versus Evolution

"Okay, Blanchie, continuing on with another big issue that we discussed for so many hours, the divine creation of the universe and man in seven days through the creation theory and then the natural evolution of the universe and man through the big bang or evolution theory?

"As far as the creation theory, we asked so many times, 'if the Earth is, give or take, four billion years old, why did God wait until fifty thousand years ago to create Adam and Eve?' You and I often contrasted this figure with scientists speculating that homo sapiens, or modern man, evolved about two hundred thousand years ago. We always saw this as a big difference time wise, and, of course, as to how man was created. One of our biggest questions was always, 'Can evolutionism and creationism be one in the same or somehow compatible?'"

"Don't forget, Bob, how Father Chuck used to bristle at even the notion of evolution? He never wanted to acknowledge the idea that creationism and evolution could in any way be compatible. Remember the time we asked him if it just might be possible that God guided, or is currently guiding, evolution in some way? He responded that the Catholic Church had no official stance on this, but he never gave us any answer. Well, I'm bound and determined to get to the bottom of this issue. Remember, Bob, how we speculated that maybe things that God created in those initial six days are now evolving on their own, without His intervention? Or that, somehow, those six days are actually part of the fourteen billion years since the birth of our universe, according to the evolution theory or part of the births of however many other universes there might be out there. Oh, Bob, remember how our heads used to swim trying to figure this one out?"

"I sure do, honey. I remember, too, at an Old Mission BBQ when Father Chuck was sitting at our table and you asked him one simple question, 'Through creationism, Adam and Eve apparently were created fully developed, just as modern humans like all of us. How would that explain the evolutionist's description of humans evolving from lower states of development to what we are today?'"

"Yes, poor Father Chuck; he suddenly got up, saying that he 'should mingle with some of the other parishioners,' anything to avoid this topic. But I think someone with the initials of Bob Fisher liked to egg him on!"

"Who, poor, little, ole me? No way, ha ha!"

"Well, Bob, it seems that this subject, like so many, does not have an automatic answer just because one is in Heaven. Hopefully I'll find out soon, as this subject is key to understanding our existence and relationship with God, Heaven, and each other! But again, Bob, I'm on it!"

sixteen

Heaven

"Okay, Honey, I guess I'm switching gears a bit. You've already told me the little you know about Heaven in the short time you've been there, especially about your immediate surroundings in SLO, but I thought I'd ask you what else you've learned about Heaven, outside of our town and outside of the United States. This was also one of the topics we discussed most—I guess because it was linked to almost every subject we discussed throughout those seventy years here on our bench and with the kids at home as they grew up. Remember our famous question based on the game show *The Price Is Right*: What's behind Door Number Three, the Afterlife?"

"Sure, Bob! First, please say grace again. There are many 'graces' that I haven't heard in a while!"

"Of course, Blanchie. You'll remember this one and Father Chuck's 'half smile' response when I told it to him: the pompous Swiss cheese executive always had a holier-than-thou attitude."

"Ha, yes, I remember that one—a real oldie but goodie, and, yes, I remember Father Chuck's reaction, as if he didn't want to acknowledge that it was a good one!

"Before we begin, remember that sharp lump in our mattress on my side of the bed that we said for years that we'd fix? It's no longer there! From what I've been told and observed, most everything in Heaven is fixed: our bodies, infrastructure, world strife, the environment, and yes, even our own mattresses!

"Well, Bob, I'm happy to continue to pass on what little I've learned about Heaven so far. But everything we discussed over the years has

62

Heaven as its common denominator, so it's going to seem like I'm jumping from one topic to another, even though they are all related to heaven!"

"I know, Blanchie, dear, just fire away; heck, I am, too, in asking you questions!"

"Okay, well, where do I start, or, really, continue, about Heaven? I've mentioned a few things already, but there is much, much more to tell you and for me to learn."

"Honey, I know a good start. Remember how we pondered how Heaven came to exist, or has it always existed, just as we learned, as Catholics, that God always was and always will be? Was Heaven created by one or more divine beings, just as we wondered if other religions had their own god or gods? This is related to the same issue as evolution versus creation—made by god or naturally occurring."

"That's right, Bob, how could I forget this issue, our biggest Heaven issue? It's on the top of my list because it elevates the whole divine versus naturally occurring debate to literally the next level, from Earth to Heaven. You and I thought it hard to believe that the creation of Heaven could have anything to do with man, yet we debated this issue a lot."

"Okay, Blanchie, moving along in our discussion of Heaven, we always wondered what happens to bad relationships on Earth when we get to Heaven and Hell: What happens with our earthly interpersonal problems? Are there any kinds of relationship issues between former spouses and their widows and widowers that remarry or not? Do victims and perpetrators of spousal and child abuse interact if the perpetrator goes to Heaven (and the same for homicide victims)? Can the victims have contact of any kind with the person or persons who killed them— the same questions for victims of torture and mass destruction, such as those from the Holocaust, Cambodia, the Crusades, etc.?

"Remember that we wondered about seeing our parents, aunts, uncles, and earthly friends in Heaven and in Hell? Well, I guess we know the answer at least to the Heaven piece!"

"Bob, these are all excellent questions that I vividly remember discussing over the years. Believe me, I'm hell-bent, so-to-speak, on getting the answers!"

"Cute, Blanchie. Just remember that bad jokes are *my* forte!"

"Many have told me that, as you and I had speculated for years, Heaven is a parallel universe of the earth that I lived on with you. Except for you, people on Earth don't realize it, but the person in Heaven can be occupying the same parallel space, like a house or, in our case, a bench, with another person on Earth, at the exact same time, like you and me on the same bench at seven a.m.! The only thing is that the person in Heaven cannot touch, see, hear, or communicate in any way with anyone on Earth, except on special occasions, which I'm told I'll learn about later. You'll be able to see and touch me when you come to Heaven!"

"Oh, yes, Blanchie, sorry to interrupt, but, is there—would there be anything you could do about that, maybe a good word or whatever?"

"Silly Bob, you definitely won't need any help in getting here, but I'll look into it anyway!

"I still don't understand how or why you and I are able to communicate, and I am not going to ask, for fear of jinxing this privilege, phenomenon, or whatever it is. It's kinda spooky when you think about it! I have discussed this with everyone in our family, that we all have occupied the same space at the same time for so many years, like sitting on the sofa or on the porch in our green Chinese house! And the funniest or spookiest thing is that neither the person on Earth nor in Heaven knows that the other person is occupying the same space!"

"Blanchie…Have they told you if there is more than one heaven? This is a subject that you and I had discussed a lot. For example, is there a heaven for each major religion and belief system, like for Christians, Muslims, Jews, Hindus, Confucianists, Taoists, Shintoists, etc.? And which subcomponents within each major religion are considered a part of these major religions; for example, are Mormons considered Christians? Oh, and are native cultures included, like the Mayans, Aztecs, Native American tribes, and the like worldwide?"

"Well, Bob, you and I were pretty much unable to figure out what each major religion's own version of Heaven would be, and now, after three days of classes and asking a million unanswered questions, I think I know why! There appears to be only one Heaven for all faiths, and it is our very own Earth, just as you and I knew it! Think about it, at least from a creationist point of view: if we are made to the image and likeness of God, who supposedly created the universe and Earth, then Earth and its inhabitants would be made in the image and likeness of God, too! This could also be true if one does not believe in God, creationism, or divine intervention of any kind, or only believes in the natural order of things, starting with the theory of evolution and the big bang theory.

"So, again, in Heaven, we all apparently continue to share this same Earth, a parallel Earth, and most everything is the same, including the exact same hours of the day and time zones throughout Earth! Here in SLO, we still have the same Jewish synagogue on Los Osos Valley Road, the Episcopal Church on Nipomo Street, the Old Mission on Chorro, the Protestant church across from Mitchell Park, and so many other beautiful houses of worship!"

"Say, Blanchie, I was just now thinking of Sister Domatilla that I had in grammar school and how she would have bristled at all this! She was so strict. I remember me and so many others getting our knuckles rapped with her eighteen-inch ruler that went with her everywhere, as if it were a part of her habit! I remember once she caught me making one of my earliest puns to some of my friends in the acoustically perfect hallway about her ever-present instrument of punishment. I remember I said, 'And when the aliens invaded Earth and came face-to-face with Sister Domatilla, they said to take them to her ruler!' She told me to outstretch my right hand and, man, did she rap those knuckles! I can still feel it—ouch!"

"Ah, yes, Bob, I remember you talking about her and that incident! Even Johnny, Mary, and Timothy had their knuckles rapped a few times by some of the nuns when they were in school. Remember when I complained to the principal, Sister Mary John, about the time our sweet Mary had her knuckles rapped? All-of-a-sudden, Sister 'What's-her-name' was working in the library. What 'nun-sense,' as you used to say! Good thing that times have changed.

"Well, getting back on the subject of Heaven and the whole issue of trying to guess and identify which denominations and sub denominations make up the world's faiths, this seems less important because they continue to exist where they were on Earth. And their members, like us Catholics, seem to come to Heaven in the same Earthly status and to have their own locally based orientation process. This would make sense if Heaven is a parallel universe to Earth. The main thing that I haven't figured out yet is how all this happens, just like all the 'how' questions that we've had for so many years!

"To illustrate this point, one of the volunteers here at orientation told me that she and her husband recently travelled to Mumbai, India, and it looked similar to when they had travelled there while on Earth, except that it had no poverty. They found out that India had a similar orientation process to ease Hindis and members of other faiths into Heaven."

"Oh, Blanchie, we talked so much about a Heaven with no class systems or poverty and no third world countries! It now seems to be true. Why can't Earth even come close to this?"

"I'm telling you Bob—you're in for a real treat! Get this: in a recent class, we learned that a poverty-stricken person who passes away on Earth stays in, or goes to, their country of origin but without the poverty! I wish I knew more about other religions in Heaven, but it seems that members of all religions are also very happy in Heaven! Apparently, any person who wants can travel to and live in any country they want! Later I'll talk about how one actually travels in Heaven."

"Oh, Blanchie, I can't wait to travel with you, Bobby, Stevie, and everyone! I guess we were so busy raising our family and being with our grands and greats that we never found the time to travel."

"Yes, Bob, and we'll have all eternity to travel! Think of all the frequent-flyer miles we'll rack up!

"Bob, you and I grew up with the strong insinuation that Catholicism was 'the one true religion.' In fact, we had talked many times about feeling sorry for non-Catholics, that they most certainly would not go to Heaven, even after living a life of hard work and following their Christian and non-Christians faiths. I think it's safe to say that, years ago, most major religions thought the same of themselves, and it has been refreshing over the years on Earth to see this notion pretty much get debunked. Now that I'm in Heaven, I believe that everyone from all religions goes to what appears to be the same Heaven and Hell on this parallel universe—or Earth—and that all persons and countries coexist peacefully and without competition! I think the absence of competition is also the key to Heaven not having an economic base and all the problems that this causes on Earth.

"I still don't know how one is chosen to go to Heaven or Hell in Catholicism or any other religion, but you know what I'm gonna say, Bob: I'm on it! This was a big topic that both of us pondered over the years!

"And, Bob, something else that you and I discussed a lot about the world's religions and cultures was that many didn't fit into the conventional denominations that we used to discuss, religions and cultures like the Mayans, Aztecs, Native American tribes, and other past and present worldwide cultures and cults. Well, as Heaven is a parallel universe, they're all here, too, located in the same countries as we all knew them, to include the current Native American tribes in the United States. This is also related to the theory of multiple gods that we speculated on so often."

"Yes, Blanchie, well, as you have said now various times, Heaven is a parallel universe to Earth, essentially the same Earth, so it would make sense that people and religions would be located in much the same places in Heaven."

"Remember, Bob, some of our other big 'Heaven' questions, most of which were interrelated:

- Is there evil in Heaven, like Lucifer, the bad angel—evil similar to that on Earth? If there is evil in Heaven, does anyone or anything combat it, and who or what is responsible evil?

- Does Lucifer exist, or any other evil forces in Heaven, and do they have any influence over anyone on Earth? Remember that comedy show in the mid-60s—oh, you know...*Laugh In*? I think it was Flip Wilson's character, Ernestine, who used to say, 'The devil made me do it!'

- Is God able to control Lucifer and his followers—either in Heaven, Hell, or on Earth—to any degree?

- And, lest we forget maybe the biggest 'Heaven' issue: Is there really any difference between my parallel universe's Heaven and the Earth that you're on? I know this sounds almost blasphemous, but think about how similar—almost identical—they both are. How much influence did/does God have in both places, as opposed to the natural order of things; you know, related to the same evolution-versus-creationism conundrum?

"Believe me, Bob, my main mission is to find out the answers to all these questions that we discussed so much over the years! I just mentioned them, so you know that I haven't forgotten! I don't think that there is any real degree of evil in Heaven—otherwise it wouldn't be Heaven, right?

"By the way, Bob, off subject again, I had mentioned before that there is a way to know on the computer if someone you knew on Earth has arrived to Heaven, something like Facebook. It only works here in Heaven for those who wish to participate. Good thing that Mary created my Facebook account on Earth, so when they explain this in tomorrow's class, it won't be a total frustration! Oh, why am I telling you all this? You never even used Facebook on Earth!"

"Facebook, Twitter—I think you and I were darn lucky to not have had to deal with all that madness as we grew up and throughout most of our adult lives!"

"Silly Bob, you're such a fuddy-duddy! I never used Twitter, but Facebook, the little that I used it, kept me younger and put me in touch with our family and friends.

"Okay, now back on track, Bob! One of the good aspects of Heaven is that people of all faiths and cultures are at peace with one another. This is one of the reasons that Heaven is so happy: there is a near complete absence of jealousy, competition, and one-upmanship! For the same reasons, there is a total lack of economic base in Heaven, and so, without money, there is no greed—just love for one another, without all the other negative byproducts of an economically based society.

"I mentioned this before, but I want to find out when man started to be known as 'man,' from either an evolutionary or creationist point of view. Science tells us that modern man, Homo sapiens, is about two hundred thousand years old and that Adam and Eve were created around the year 4005 BC, another big disparity in the whole evolution-versus-creation theories. And so, as you and I discussed so many times, when did man, Homo sapiens, start to go to Heaven and Hell, despite his religion or lack thereof, as would have been the case in both of these scenarios?

"By the way, Bob, we have a class on Hell tomorrow! Should be a hot topic. Get it, Bob…a hot topic?"

"Got it, Blanchie. I'll take care of the bad jokes, if you don't mind!"

"Oh, Bob, believe me. I remember all these issues, and I'm doing my best to get answers!"

"Believe me, Blanchie, I know. The way I see it, there's really no hurry, and you and I will certainly soon be able to do our 'sleuthing' together when—or maybe, if—I arrive to Heaven!"

"Silly Bob, of course we'll be together at some point, and yes, I would love to continue our discussions and investigations here with you in Heaven!

"On a similar subject, Bob, yesterday I talked to a man who claimed to have been an atheist on Earth, so I suppose that atheists come to the same Heaven that I'm in! All those years of us Catholics and Christians thinking that believing in God, and, more specifically, accepting Jesus Christ as our Lord and Savior was a prerequisite to going to Heaven, gives one pause to think! Remember Eva Andre, our dear sweet 'Daily Masser' friend, as you and I called her? The other day I asked her, 'Doesn't it irk you that you went to the seven a.m. mass every day, said the rosary afterward, wore your scapulars and medals, hung your Sacred Heart and Blessed Virgin Mary pictures on the wall at the entrance to your house, and said multitudes of novenas and prayer cards, and here's Joe Blow the atheist right here next to you in Heaven?'

"She just laughed and said, 'No!'

"Oh, and, Bob, this atheist I talked to still doesn't believe in God, so I think that, even in Heaven, there's at least some degree of doubt about God's existence! This makes me wonder if I'll ever see or meet him, and why, even in Heaven, there seems to be an air of mystery surrounding the physical existence of God the Father, God the Son, God the Holy Spirit, the Blessed Virgin Mary, the saints, and the angels. Oh, Bob, I don't mean to sound negative. I'm sure everything will be revealed in due time, just certainly not during this orientation week. What sorta concerns me is that even long-term residents of Heaven aren't able to answer most of my questions, either, leading me to contemplate never finding answers to our questions."

"Well, Blanchie, you just keep being nosy about all these important issues, just like those TV magazine shows that we both used to watch! You'll get to the bottom of these topics!"

"Sure, Bob!

"Remember how we sometimes wondered if there were social classes in Heaven? From what I can gather, there aren't, as you might expect. Remember the volunteers here at orientation that I just mentioned? They said the same thing about Mumbai, India—that they saw no poverty there. Here in SLO and nearby, there are many former famous people living. Again, in Heaven there is no jealousy, no monetary system, and no class system. If one meets someone who was famous on Earth, it's no big thing. I guess it's hard to explain, just like how people who, on Earth, had bad relationships but don't in Heaven."

"Bob, I want to add to something that I mentioned a bit ago about there being no social classes. There are no homeless people in Heaven. In the case of a famous entertainer on Earth, for example, he or she can continue to entertain, but they no longer have this superstar status. They entertain because they just want to, like anyone who works in Heaven. On TV the other night, I saw Bob Hope, my all-time favorite on Earth, do a forty-five minute standup routine that made me split a gut! It's the same with former sports stars—say baseball players, like in the movie *Field of Dreams*—who play just for the fun of it!

"Bob, we've never discussed this, but you've told me many times that *Field of Dreams* is one of your favorite movies. I know this is a sensitive subject for you, but maybe you've fantasized about having a 'catch' with your dad when you come to Heaven? Bob? Oh, Bob, please don't cry! Bob?"

"Blanchie, you've touched on my most sensitive, personal secret, one that I haven't even told you! You are so perceptive! Yes, *Field of Dreams* is my favorite movie because it touches my life and my heart. Yes, I have often thought about having a catch with my dad, a chance to make up for all my childhood years of no meaningful contact with him. I have never stopped fantasizing about that moment and what I would say to him. If you don't mind, could we talk about this later?"

"Sure, Bob, but your relationship with your dad is something that you could never hide from me. It has been written on your forehead all these years!

"Well, continuing on, we had a class yesterday about how things get done, or simply how Heaven works. Remember that Heaven is a parallel universe to Earth, so you might well ask who cleans the streets, runs the stores, fixes the roof leaks, drives the busses and ambulances—who runs the day-to-day, nitty-gritty stuff just like on Earth? And what is anyone's incentive to do so? Because there's no money in Heaven, and everything is provided.

"From the class and the little time I've been here in Heaven, Bob, it appears that everyone who wants to work does so voluntarily, as I kinda just mentioned with the celebrities' example. Think about it: everyone is basically retired, right? After a while one wants to contribute, so, voilà, there's your work pool!"

"That's so interesting, Blanchie, and a subject I don't remember discussing much, but it fits with this theme of demystifying most aspects of the afterlife and religion that we discussed for so many years—and now, hopefully, are getting closer to understanding.

"Blanchie, another question related to Heaven that you and I discussed over the years: What is a soul? You and I were taught that when one died on Earth, his or her soul went to Heaven, or in the other direction! But we agreed that we never fully understood what a soul was. Have they covered this in your classes yet?"

"Well, Bob, yes, a little, but I have to admit that I still don't understand. As we learned in our classes, the soul is real but has no form and is our most basic 'life force,' our energy that allows us to live, breathe, think, and to be human on Earth and in Heaven. Remember we were taught in catechism classes as kids that when we die on Earth, our souls are transported to Heaven and we take on the same human form in Heaven that we had on Earth. And no, Bob, I haven't yet found out how our souls are transported, either. How many times did we ask that question over the years?"

"I'll say! And, Blanchie, the saints were a big part of our religious upbringing and the subject of many, many hours of discussion on our bench! And, since it's a subject related to Heaven, what have you learned about them?"

"Ah, Bob, that's another great topic that we have touched on at orientation, but only a little bit.

"I guess I can sum it up this way: most religions believe to some degree in either saints or other revered and holy individuals, including Buddhists, Hindus, Sikhs, Protestants, and Roman and Greek Orthodox

Catholics. Our questions over the years dealt with the so-called Catholic saints, so I'll share what little I've learned in my classes, but there has been very little outside the Catholic perspective. I hope to find persons of these other faiths and ask them these and all of our questions!

"I've learned that Protestant—that is, non-Catholic Christians—theology teaches that anyone who has accepted Jesus Christ as Lord and Savior becomes, at that moment, a saint, regardless of his or her church or social standing. So, in the Protestant faiths, it is impossible to calculate how many saints there are, because we cannot know exactly how many people have accepted Jesus Christ as their Lord and Savior.

"Now, Bob, as you know, in the Catholic faith, things are more formal. We know about the process and road to sainthood, which Pope John Paul II streamlined in 1983. In Catholicism, we learned that there have been over ten thousand official saints over history, but no exact number. Hey, Bob, remember Butler's *Lives of the Saints* that we made the kids read every day? Turns out that it is still the most definitive book about the saints!

"And I still kid my mom about her multitude of prayer cards that she faithfully recited at five p.m. every day, just after saying the rosary! Guess what, Bob? Old habits die hard; she still does this!"

"Our mothers are perfect examples of how everyone uses the term 'saint' to refer to a person, living or not, as very good and righteous—one who has dedicated his or her life to the service of others. These persons don't end up being officially recognized as 'saints,' but…they are!"

"Amen, Bob, amen!

"Okay, so our real questions about the saints were always: Who are they? Where are they, and what do they do day to day? In some of our classes, saints were defined as physical human beings in Heaven who have been honored through the processes of beatification and canonization, as opposed to angels, who are not human beings, yet are created by God and serve as messengers or on special projects.

"Now, as to where saints live, what they do day to day, and how they interact with the Holy Trinity, the rest of us in Heaven, the angels, and those of you on Earth haven't been told. Believe me, Bob, I'm really trying to demystify as much as I can about the afterlife, and again, I'm on it!

"Bob, I should get going. I don't want to get in trouble for being late to class! I love you so much! I so wish you didn't have to come to Heaven to see and touch me, but I want you to continue to enjoy our kids, grands, and greats as long as you can!"

"I love you too, Blanchie! We'll talk in the morning! Oh, by the way, is it possible for us to have an argument, me on our bench and you in Heaven?"

"Silly Bob, we never really argued on our bench all those years, did we? Well, seems it's almost impossible to get into an argument in Heaven, but maybe we could pretend to have one if you want to argue from Earth!

Okay, today we'll learn about Hell. Tomorrow's chat with you should be very interesting!"

"It should, indeed, Blanchie; have a great day!"

o

seventeen

Hell

"Good morning, Blanchie. I think yesterday you had your class on 'the other place'! I'm dying—well, maybe just very curious—to know what you found out about it!"

"Ha, Bob! You mean Hell! First, would you please say grace?"

"Of course, Honey. I keep forgetting! Let's see. You've heard all of them, but here's one that fits our current discussion: the easygoing Satanist had a devil-may-care attitude."

"Ah, yes, Bob, I remember that one. It always made me laugh!

"Well, Bob, this is not my favorite topic, either! Remember that Heaven is a parallel universe to Earth. Yesterday I learned that Hell is located here in Heaven, specifically, in each country where the person died, regardless of one's religious affiliation. I learned that each religion in each country is responsible for its own version of Hell, but my class focused on the United States.

"And no, silly Bob, Hell has nothing to do with fire!"

"Go on, Honey; this is gonna be interesting."

"Actually, it is, Bob, and my eyes were opened up really wide as this whole subject was greatly demystified. Seems that Hell, at least in the United States, is located in the existing federal or state penitentiaries, called Hell Prisons or HPs for short, and run by the same federal or state entities that ran them on Earth. In the United States, our federal HPs continue to be run by the Federal Bureau of Prisons, and the states' are run by the individual State Bureaus of Prisons.

"I don't know exactly how they are operated in other countries, but they are all incredibly well run, as there have been very few escapes

Heaven-wide. So, yes, I suppose there is evil in Heaven; maybe a controlled evil, where Hell is completely separated from the rest of Heaven."

"Oh, Blanchie, tell me what goes on inside the prison walls, inside Hell. Is there parole, or do inmates' cases get overturned? What incentive is there for a prisoner to behave him or herself, knowing that they will be in prison for all eternity? I have so many other questions about Hell."

"Whoa, slow down, cowboy! I know what your questions are; remember that we discussed them on our bench for so many years!

"What goes on behind those prison walls, you ask? Well, Jim, a guard, spoke to us yesterday in our class. He works at HP23, in the former federal prison at Lompoc, California. He was a guard at the same prison for thirty-two years, and, as so many others, 'returned' as a guard after he died, just because he enjoyed the job. He said that HPs are similar to the federal and state prisons on Earth but more unpleasant and unhappy, because, as you said, the inmates know that they now have no chance to get out and will remain there for all eternity.

"According to Jim, HPs worldwide are a big deal, with about ten million prisoners incarcerated at any given time. Currently, there are one million prisoners in US federal and state prisons, followed by Russia and China, but Jim didn't know their figures. Nearly eighty new federal and state HPs have been built over the last fifty years to ease the overcrowding of prisons in Heaven. As I said, all new and existing prisons are so well built and guarded that escapes are very rare. With more prisons, there is a bigger guard-to-prisoner ratio."

"Blanchie, just as you and I discussed for so many years, my next questions are: What are the crimes on my Earth that will get someone sent to Hell? And who decides who goes to Hell?"

"Bob, just as I couldn't answer the same question about who decides who goes to Heaven, I can't answer this one, either, except to say that, just as when someone goes to Heaven, one's soul is transported to Hell, too.

"Your other question was if anyone ever leaves the HPs on any kind of parole or if their case is overturned on appeal?

"The answer seems to be no, according to Jim. Entering into Heaven seems to be rather generously granted, but getting out of Hell is not, as residents of Hell have truly 'earned their way' there. There seem to be no appeals per se.

"On this note, I don't understand what, if any, legal processes there are for residents of Hell, or if there are any legal processes at all—if maybe they are a combination of divine and human justice. This point has everything to do with our long-standing discussion of Heaven being run by God, humans, or maybe both. Remember how we speculated about Heaven being a parallel universe and now it appears to be just that? But we also wondered just who 'ran' Heaven, especially the day-to-day aspects, just like on Earth. I just explained what I think are the economic and work aspects of Heaven—that people come back to work because they want to—but who, really, is in charge in Heaven? On Earth one can easily say that each country is autonomous, but what about in Heaven? I haven't even been told yet if the United States or any other country has a president. I'm desperately trying to find out the divine role in the operation of Heaven and how it coincides with the human role. My guess is that Heaven was created by one or more divine beings and that we residents run the day-to-day stuff, just like on Earth.

"This is also related to our previous conundrum of who determines who goes to Heaven or Hell."

"Blanchie, all this is so interesting! Now, do murder victims or their families in Heaven ever have contact with their killers?"

"Ah, Bob, excellent question! Yes, according to Jim, HPs offer the victims and their families the chance for this to happen under very, very tight security and only when the victims and their families agree. These visits are very rare, but when they happen, they occur in the typical scenario of bulletproof-glass booths with the perpetrator on one side, handcuffed in leg irons, and the victim on the other. They can speak out loud through built-in microphones, and three guards stand three feet away. Of course, the victims are transported to the HP and then back to Heaven, just as they did on Earth if they visited the perpetrator in a federal or state prison.

"Jim described the meeting between a female murderer and her victims, a famous Hollywood actress, her forty-three-year-old son who died in utero as a result of being stabbed numerous times, and three other victims in a Los Angeles murder spree.

"Interestingly, the actress and her son forgave the woman, who, during her thirty-seven years in prison, apologized to the families involved and became a born-again Christian. It appears, though, that this wasn't enough to save her from an eternity in Hell, which also calls into question the notion of going to Heaven if one truly accepts Jesus as Lord and Savior."

"Yes, Honey, I remember those murders. I believe that you, I, and the kids were heading back home after a Dodger game against the Cubs when the news came over the radio. I think it was in August of 1969, and all of LA was horrified and on edge. Remember how you wished that our car could go faster so we could get out of LA quicker?"

"Oh, Bob, that was an awful drive home, and I remember turning the car radio off so we would not hear any more news flashes on this horrific event.

"Again, this brings up the interesting point about forgiveness in Heaven. Seems that it doesn't always exist, although forgiveness is the rule rather than the exception, as opposed to on Earth. So, yes, Bob, it does appear that there can be bad feelings in Heaven to varying degrees.

"But, Bob, here's another example on a larger scale. In our class about Hell, we saw footage of a second Nuremberg trial held about ten years ago, in which Hitler and his top henchmen were retried over a period of seven days in a large local stadium that seated fifty thousand concentration camp victims from all over the world, but mostly from Europe. Seats were reserved through a type of lottery system. The remaining millions of victims, families, and Heaven-wide residents were able to witness this event on TV.

"It was so, so emotional, and many say cathartic, for millions of Jews who were slaughtered and gassed in those horrific camps to see Hitler and his conspirators, and to know that their fate was, in fact, eternal damnation!"

"Wow, Blanchie, no one on Earth, of course, had any idea!

"Okay, Blanchie, you knew this question was coming: What have you heard about the devil? Does he exist? What is his power or influence both in Heaven and on Earth? Where does he live? How many followers does he have?"

"Ah, Bob, how many times did we discuss this specific topic! I'll tell you that answers to this subject are the same as to the subject of God; I simply don't know yet! You and I were taught that the devil is the former angel Lucifer who fell from God's graces. But I have learned in these classes that angels are not real persons, like residents of Heaven and the saints.

"There's also the whole issue of his followers—how many are there, and how do they operate from, I suppose, their HPs, like gangs here on Earth, if that's where they are? Or maybe they're bad angels and therefore not human, and maybe harder to control. I have to say that the answer is probably going to be along the lines that Lucifer and his cohorts are somehow greatly controlled and, therefore, are basically ineffective in negatively influencing residents and life in Heaven."

"Okay, Blanchie, and as you and I dwelled on for so many years, there is the question of any influence or direct control by the devil and his followers over those of us on Earth, not just in Heaven. Are they, let's say, responsible, at least in part, for some or all of the evil on Earth? How do they spread evil, especially if they are so tightly controlled in HPs all over the world?"

"Remember, Bob, that we often speculated that the devil is another term for our human failings and horrific compulsions, that he didn't really physically exist?"

"Okay, Blanchie, tell me: Is there devil's food or angel food cake in Heaven?"

"Most silly Bob, yes. There are both kinds, and in fact, that reminds me: I'll make both tonight. Remember the two Betty Crocker mixes in the pantry? They're still there! Your favorite was always devil's food cake!"

"Okay, Blanchie, this conversation has given me a hankering for some devil's food cake! Since my personal chef isn't here, guess I'll run over to Skolari's or Ralf's supermarkets and buy one already made! Howzabout we stop here and continue on in the morning?"

"Sounds like a plan, Stan! Oh, Bob, how I miss you and love you! I don't have any 'intel' on this, but I'm selfishly hoping that we're together sooner than later!"

"Me, too, Blanchie, me too!"

eighteen

Eternity

"Good morning, Honey, got your coffee in tow?"

"In tow? Have you gone navy on me, Bob? I don't know about 'in tow,' but I have my usual Pete's dark roast with my cream and Splenda. Yes, silly Bob, we have Splenda here in Heaven. I use it, I guess, out of habit. Now that I can't die again, there's no real need to watch what I eat and drink!

"Okay, so maybe start us off with some grace?"

"Let's see, now; let me see. Okay, remember this one: 'The confused navigator, passing between Alaska and Russia, stopped to get his Bering Strait. Before you stop laughing, here's another one: The idea of a fifty-yard sprint for 'follicley' challenged men is pure balderdash."

"Ha, Bob, yes, I remember those! I miss your clever puns, and I hope you'll never stop making them here in Heaven! Well, wait, let me first see if there's a list of behaviors on Earth that will get one barred from entry."

"Funny and cute, Honey.

"Well, we also talked a lot about eternity on our bench. Remember how we tried to define it and relate it to the concept that God always was and always will be? We also tried to describe it in terms of simple time, but I think we just plain couldn't ever define eternity."

"Ah, yes, Bob, eternity! Well, I'm not gonna break my streak here and define or describe it here, either!

"The definition of eternity, as we learned it on Earth and here in my classes, is unchanged; it is still defined as 'endless time'—time that never started and will never end, mirroring the concept that God always existed, that he had no beginning and that he will have no end. As you said and as we talked about for so many years, though, there does not seem to be any scientific evidence of eternity. But remember, Bob, I'm Detective Blanchie!

"Since I arrived, I've been told not to stress out about eternity or worry about being, let's say, 'stuck,' in a geographic location or in any situation forever, as we can change all this as much as we want here in Heaven.

"Well, now to the facts that I think I know about time in Heaven. Time is the same here in Heaven, Bob, each minute consisting of sixty seconds, each hour of sixty minutes, each day of twenty-four hours, and each year of three hundred and sixty-five days! Heaven has all the same time zones, too, as on Earth. To me, I don't feel and different time-wise.

"Growing up and even as adults, Bob, you and I were, I guess, led to believe that eternity was something unimaginable, indescribable, and something we would only understand when we got there—well, 'here,' for me! But, like many things we've been discussing this past week, it's really not like this at all!

"I have not seen or heard of any scientific evidence of what eternity is in my one week here in Heaven, but then, in some or even most cases, Heaven is not a place that is based on science! Yes, the universe appears to be about fourteen billion years old, but I have not heard of, or seen any, scientific evidence of this universe never having had a beginning, nor that it will have an end. From a religious point of view, as Catholics, you and I were always taught about the existence of eternity, and, like so many other dogmas, it was implied that we never question it. Bob, believe me, I'm trying to find out how all Christian and non-Christian religions and science explain eternity, and all of the issues we've discussed in the past few days and throughout those years on our bench!

"Bob, I guess the good news and the main point here is that eternity means that we will enjoy Heaven for longer than we can even imagine, and that this is a good thing, with no bad aspects to it!"

"Well, when you put it that way, Honey, it is not so important to know exactly what eternity is!"

"One last thing on the subject of eternity, I just had a chilling thought: Bob, please don't bring your snoring when you get here, okay?"

"Well, Blanchie, there's no one here on Earth anymore to shake me when I snore. Maybe I don't snore anymore!"

"Fat chance, Señor Snore!

nineteen

Judgment Day, Purgatory and Limbo

"Say, Bob, remember how we were always taught as Catholics that we would be judged on Judgment Day, on the last day of Earth's existence, then sent to Heaven, Hell, Purgatory, or Limbo, right?

"From what I can see and have been told, I have arrived directly to Heaven, and I haven't experienced any kind of judgment process. Oh, Bob, I'm told that I'm in Heaven, so I'm kind of hesitant to ask any questions until much later in this process, so as to not be told, 'Oh, Blanche Tate Fisher, you don't belong here; we're going to send you to…' Ha!

"I'm getting the idea that probably neither Purgatory nor Limbo exists. Our classes have been noncommittal one way or the other. Starting with Limbo, this always seemed to be a vague, undefined state and location where, you and I were taught, unbaptized babies and unbaptized humans of any age or religion went while they awaited their 'final fate,' because they still had Original Sin.

"Get this, Bob, breaking news related to Limbo: For Catholics, at least, it also seems that there is no Original Sin, a controversial subject since the second century when the term was invented. Original Sin was believed by many to be due to Adam and Eve's first sin in the Garden of Eden, and a condition inherited by all humans, only removed through Christ dying on the cross and through baptism. Remember how lucky we always felt we had been baptized and 'those poor babies and adults that weren't?' Also, you and I always thought that it was so unfair for all of us Christians to be the innocent victims of Adam and Eve having eaten of the forbidden fruit!"

"I'll say, Honey! I certainly hope that what you say about Limbo and Original Sin is correct! We had speculated as much on our bench."

"Bob, kinda related to Limbo and Purgatory, there was another topic that we always discussed, too, about where people of any religion went, you know, Heaven or Hell, before Christ died on the cross, because there was no Christianity before Christ, and thus no Christians to be saved.

Similarly, you and I often talked about if Heaven even existed for Christians before Christ died on the cross, and for anyone of any religion. We also wondered at what point did Heaven begin to exist in all religions? Remember, too, Bob, how we spent so many hours wondering if there was, or is, a similar process in all religions to be selected to go to Heaven or Hell? This all goes back to the question, 'is there more than one God?' Believe me, Bob, I'm hot on the trail of these answers!"

"Oh, Blanchie, you know that, over the years, we never really sat down and discussed all these issues at once, like we basically are now, so all this is kinda overwhelming!"

"Tell me about it, buddy! How do you think I feel?

Now for Purgatory. You and I were taught that it is a vague place of purification or temporary punishment if a Christian dies in the 'state of grace'—in other words, without any mortal sins. No one has been able to confirm if Purgatory is still in effect, and, if so, what and where it is or was located. Here at orientation, I've gotten a lot of vague answers again, which suggests to me that the Catholic Church is not sure, either. Bob, remember how afraid we were of going there? Hey, the fact that I skipped out on Sunday mass so many times without an excuse in and of itself a mortal sin, and the fact that I am here in Heaven might answer the question about the existence of Purgatory, dontcha think?"

"Hey, girl, don't think you had the 'skipping Sunday mass' thing cornered! As a kid, I could have been hired as a 'mass-skipping consultant.'"

"Remember we were told that Purgatory was a mass of flames, and we had to endure them for as long as it took to make up for our sins on Earth, so we would enter into Heaven with a clean slate, so to speak? I remember as a third grader just shaking with fright in catechism classes when this subject was mentioned!"

"Believe me, Blanchie, you weren't the only one shaking in those catechism classes!

"Okay, so, let me get this straight. When we die, we either go to Heaven or Hell; is that it? No intermediate stops, so to speak, like Purgatory or Limbo? Hmm, just think of the naughty things I coulda done, and still can!"

"Okay, Bob, don't get carried away! Yes, it would appear that we all go to one place or the other after we die on Earth, at least as Christians. One of our instructors put it this way: 'Everyone on Earth is a sinner, but only those who committed the very worst crimes, whether or not they were convicted in a court of law on Earth, will most certainly go to Hell.' Oh, Bob, again, no one can tell how this process works, including who makes this decision or how it's made, and no one, student or instructor, seems to want to delve any further for fear of stirring the pot!

"Bob, I touched on the concept of Judgment Day a second ago, and I'd like to go back to it. This is another subject that the instructors seem to need further training on, as I and others have asked rather direct questions, only to meet with vague responses."

"Yes, Blanchie, this concept was always somewhat vague and difficult to understand, and, in catechism, hard for the teachers to explain. I seem to remember that Judgment Day appears a lot in the Bible, especially in Matthew's Gospels."

"Bob, remember we were taught that the Nicene Creed said, in part, 'He, Jesus Christ, will come again in glory to judge the living and the dead.' No one ever explained to you and me just how and when we would be judged, leading most Catholics, and I suppose most Protestants, too, to speculate that everyone, at least all Christians, would be judged at the end of the world. Of course, no one ever knew, or knows, when the end of the world on Earth will be, or even if there will be an end to the world. And, for sure, no one here seems to know anything about what an end to the world on Earth would be like.

"So, Bob, since I and everyone else here in Heaven, including all Catholics and Protestants, seem to have arrived immediately after our passings on Earth, it would appear that there is no Judgment Day for Catholics and Protestants. I've spoken with the instructors at this orientation course and with so many of our friends, and this seems to be the case! It would appear that we earn our entrance into Heaven or Hell while on Earth.

"I feel bad for the instructors because they are unable to answer most of our questions. I suppose that we'll find out over time and that our orientation is not a forum to answer these tough questions."

"Honey, I know you don't know, but we discussed this issue so many years: In case there were some kind of judgment for Catholics and Christians in general, who judges us? Christ, God the Father, or God the Holy Spirit? Who judges members of the rest of the world's religions, all the atheists, and those who just have no formal religion, and what's the process? This all gets back to our major questions about if each religion has its own god and how many gods there are.

"Let's not forget the time and logistics involved in judging everyone, whoever gets judged, Christian or not, which, along with all of our questions over the years, are real 'demystifying' issues!

"I know, Blanchie, you don't know but you're working on it!"

"Well, Bob, you're right! In addition to what you just said, remember that we wondered what the end of the world is, and what does it mean that God will come again to judge the living and the dead? These topics aren't at all clear, especially the whole idea of being judged. Remember, since I've come to Heaven, I've been asking these and so many other questions, like: Does praying work? Who answers our prayers, if anyone? Why do we pray for the deceased, and does this increase their chances of going 'north or south'? But, Bob, I'm going to find out…Just give me more time here to feel comfortable asking these types of questions, which, in a Catholic environment here at orientation, are not easy to ask! Just about everyone I talk to doesn't want to really contemplate any of the questions that you and I discussed for so many years! I think that most people feel disloyal if they ask any questions that might seem even remotely contradictory to their faith. But, Bob, I think this is changing, because I really haven't gotten any negative reactions to most of these questions so far, at least among my friends!

twenty

The Four Gospels

"Well, Blanchie, my dear, speaking of negative reactions, we discussed many time the accuracy of the four New Testament Gospels which you and I and all Christians have kinda taken as, well, 'Gospel,' believing that four Gospels could, in fact, be God's word. We even stand in Mass for the Gospel readings. This topic fits with most, really, all of our topics, in that so little is known about it and remains very mysterious.

"Have you learned anything about this issue?"

"Aha, Bob, you know how to pick the controversial subjects! Just kidding! I know we talked about this subject many times, and I remember when you brought it up with Father Chuck—I thought he was going to twist and turn and writhe on the floor!"

"Well, as you might expect, this topic is not discussed, and the four Gospels are, as they say, taken for 'Gospel,' not discussed or analyzed. I'll tell you that I plan to follow up on the following points that you and I discussed over the years.

"The historical reliability of the Gospels, which we decided was the reliability and historic accurateness of the four New Testament gospels. Are they historically accurate? Some allege that all four gospels while others say that little in the Gospels is historically reliable.

Modern scholars agree that Jesus existed, but others are at odds as far as specific events in the Bible regarding Jesus, saying that the only two events universally agreed are that Jesus was baptized by John the Baptist and that He was crucified by the order of Pontius Pilate. Historical aspects of authenticity in dispute include the two accounts of the Nativity of Jesus, as well as the resurrection and various details about the crucifixion.

"Oh, Blanchie, how many times did we include this subject in our discussions about the many unknown and mysterious things about God?"

"Yes, Bob, believe me, I'm determined to find out more this and all subjects that we discussed for over seventy years!

"Well, according to one of my classes and what we were taught on Earth, the four Gospels are the primary sources of historical information about Jesus and of Christianity that he founded. The first three Gospels—Matthew, Mark, and Luke—recount the life, ministry, crucifixion and resurrection of Jesus. The fourth Gospel, John, is supposed to be very different from the first three.

"Remember in our adult catechism classes, we also learned that historians often look at the historical reliability of the Acts of the Apostles when studying the reliability of the Gospels, as they are seemingly written by the same author as the Gospel of Luke, although apparently there are passages in Acts that contradict Luke. There are different opinions as to the origin of the texts. Bob, in catechism, we were taught that the Gospels of the New Testament were written in Greek for Greek-speaking communities that were later translated into Syriac, Latin, and Coptic, adding to possible confusion and compromised authenticity.

"Bob, remember that we were also taught that historians have critically analyzed the Gospels, trying to differentiate authentic, reliable information from possible exaggerations and inaccurate changes. I learned that the Gospels' manuscripts include many variations, and because of this, scholars have a hard time determining which variations were original. We learned that to answer these questions, scholars have to ask who wrote the Gospels, when they wrote them, what was their purpose was in writing them, what sources the authors used, how reliable these sources were, and how far removed in time the sources were from the events they describe.

"Apparently, scholars can also look into the internal evidence of the documents, to see if, for example, the document is making claims about geography that were incorrect, or if the author appears to be hiding embarrassing information. Finally, scholars turn to external sources, including the testimony of early church leaders, writers outside the church (mainly Jewish and Greco-Roman historians) who would have been more likely to criticize the church and any archaeological evidence."

"Wow, Blanchie, you are definitely up on this topic that we talked about so much! Remember how we felt like we were disloyal, even blasphemous, to the Catholic Church just by discussing this and most of our topics?"

"Yes, Bob, I do, but, again, we never meant it that way! We were just being curious about this and all the rest of our topics. Okay, what should we talk about next?"

twenty one

Earl's Suicide

"Well, Blanchie, I think this next topic fits in with our previous discussion of Judgment Day and Purgatory. We often talked about the subject of suicide, remember? It always seemed unfair that people who committed suicide would automatically go to Hell, as we were taught most of our lives, especially in our catechism class. Over the years we often said that some people had their reasons for committing suicide—that maybe they were under a lot of stress and temporarily were in a vulnerable emotional state, and that some might have been in so much physical pain that they saw no other way out.

"Remember when Johnny found our neighbor, Earl, dead in his bed from a self-inflicted gunshot back in sixty-four? Has the subject of suicide come up in your orientation classes?"

"Yes, my dearest Bob, we discussed suicide many times, didn't we? As Catholics, you and I were always brought up to believe that suicide was a mortal sin and that those who committed it went to Hell, I guess regardless of the circumstances.

"I know a big question we also had was how can missing mass and committing suicide be the same mortal sin? But that issue is for another time, I suppose!

"In one of our classes, suicide was discussed at length. It seems that the Catholic Church has revised its stance on suicide—that it is no longer a mortal sin because the motive behind it is, as you and I had also speculated so often, almost always related to a person acting in an irrational way, again due to mental illness. In Earl's case, I have great news! He's here in Heaven and still lives on Palm Street, just in another house! He's fine and says hi! I looked him up and spoke with him yesterday when I went to his house just to see if he was still living there!

"He confirmed what we had thought, that he was depressed in his navy retirement and felt hostage to his crutches from when he got the Benz as a deep sea diver. He had no family or friends, just us to talk to occasionally. He said he became despondent when told he'd have to move out of his house. I guess his aunt actually owned it, but for some reason, she did not leave it to him when she died. He said he had nowhere to go when told that the house was to be demolished to make way for a professional office building. Two days before Johnny found him in bed, he had apparently wrapped a small gun in a towel and shot himself in bed, so none of us heard anything. Good thing Johnny went to check up on him. With Johnny being only nineteen, I was worried that finding Earl would leave emotional scars on him. Obviously it didn't!

"Well, from what I've learned at this orientation, Earl is one type of case where one is looking to escape a 'living hell on Earth' because of emotional, mental, or physical problems, or combinations of the same. Here in Heaven, many have committed suicide on Earth because they didn't want to burden their families as they started losing control of their mental or physical capacities through Alzheimer's or cancer. But, Bob, there are other suicides that are related to major crimes, such as when a murderer takes his own life to avoid arrest or prison, in which the murder is the event that usually sends this person to Hell. Again, Bob, I don't know what the process is for determining who goes to Heaven or Hell.

"Bob, directly related to this subject of suicide, I have talked to a few people here in Heaven who took their lives. It's interesting and adds a whole new dimension to this subject, both legally on Earth and religiously here in Heaven!"

"Oh, yes, Honey! Remember, too, that we saw a special on TV about an organization that assists those who want to escape their physical and emotion suffering. What was it called—Final Departure, I think? Have you heard anything on the Catholic Church's stance on suicide, especially assisted suicide?"

"Yes, Bob, that's right. Three days ago in my classes, I talked to James and Trudy, not related to each other, but who admitted taking their lives in separate incidents by inhaling helium-filled bags that they placed over their heads, which suffocated them, even though they didn't feel like they were suffocating. They told me that this is becoming a very common way of voluntarily 'departing' Earth, and that several organizations, like the one you just mentioned, are dedicated to this and other forms of 'assisted suicide.' They said that this is considered a humane form of exiting Earth when one is overwhelmed by the above-mentioned suffering.

"Now, Bob, you asked about the Catholic Church's stance on suicide, especially assisted suicide. I cannot get any of the instructors to even speculate on these issues, which basically tells me that the church's stance has not changed—that it still considers suicide a mortal sin. This, however, doesn't seem to jive with the presence of Earl, James, Trudy, and so many others that took their own lives but are here in Heaven."

"I suppose so, Blanchie. Please stay on this issue and the other big one of who judges or determines where someone goes who commits suicide, Heaven or Hell. We can also add the same question regarding anyone who assists someone else in their 'final departure,' as well as group cult suicides like that one in San Diego in 1997."

"Yes, Bob, I have the same questions, and, as I've said, I'm on it!"

"Okay, Bob, I have to get going to my class! I'm not complaining, but I have a feeling that I'm going to learn more from asking questions of our friends outside of classes."

"Okay, Blanchie. I miss you so much! Please give my love to everyone, especially your parents, Speeder, Bobby, and Stevie! Tell them how much I love them and wait for the happy, happy day when I'll see you and everyone!"

"Silly Bob, I always do! I'll see you tomorrow! I miss you, and I love you too!"

twenty two

Angels

"Good morning, Blanchie! I got my Pete's coffee, one of these new-fangled mochaccino coffees—not too bad. You know me, not much on change, so I think I'll stick to my good old-fashioned Dark Roast!"

"Well, Bob, good for you! Go ahead, go out on that limb…Live on the edge…Push that envelope! I have my coffee in hand, too. I went to Pete's on Higuera Street right before coming here! It's nice to go and not have to pay those outrageous prices! How you and I loved going there! Best cap in town! Well, remember Ole Charlie who was a regular every morning and then passed? Guess who's working there and served me this morning? He still has the same bright smile, and he'll tell you an occasional joke! He asked about you, and I told him you were 'on deck,' to borrow a baseball term, and thinking of our dear Dodgers!"

"That's great, Blanchie! I know you can't tell him hi for me, but I'll probably see him sooner than later, if you catch my drift!

"Okay, Honey, here is today's grace: the day after Christmas, I was taken aback by all the gifts that were being returned!"

"Ah, yes, Mr. Notorious Punster, that was one of my favorites! Kinda goes with one of your pre-Christmas puns, something about the department store employees preparing customers' gifts while listening to wrap music.

"Say, Bob Fisher, howzabout another grace?"

"Sure, Honey, and I have just the one: 'The two podiatrists entered the convention to see what was a foot.' Or how about this one that Father Chuck never liked: 'The church secretary's boss was so mean to her that he appeared anticlerical.'"

"Ha, Bob, yes, those were also two good ones!"

"You know, Blanchie, you should be thankful for my daily bombardments with puns over the years; they earned you your Purple Heart and most certainly helped you get into Heaven!"

"Well, my dearest, moving on, and since we're not following any particular order, we often discussed angels—who they are, where they live, and what their functions are.

"In a previous orientation class, we were taught that angels are one of God's first creations, maybe created on the second or fifth day, and that they are a separate species, spirits with no real bodies. They never have been, and never will be, human, even though they can take on human form according to the needs of the mission they're on. Oh, and Bob, I'm told that angels don't have wings, which goes against so many images that we had seen during our lives. I want to find out how angels came to be portrayed with wings!

"I asked one question that the instructors couldn't answer: Do angels die or somehow cease to exist, and are new angels born or created from time to time?

"And, Bob, to answer your next question, I haven't seen an angel yet, but in my classes, I've learned that they are the same as when we discussed them on the bench—that angels are messengers, often appearing in human form, sending people on Earth advice, information, comfort, and protection in many ways. They are sent on specific missions, such as to cheer people up, to send messages directly or indirectly in human form, to protect certain areas and people on Earth who believe in them, and so on. And no, Bob, I don't know who creates, picks, and sends them on their missions, nor who picks the missions or how they find out about them. Believe me, I don't understand most things about angels! As I just said, they look like real human beings, but they aren't. And they aren't always good, as we saw with Satan and many other fallen angels. So, Bob, this "angels" class, quite frankly, was kinda academic and boring as we learned about the different types of angels and what they are associated with, although it wasn't explained how each type of angel is employed. I think I won't bore you with the specifics!

"One question we always had was not confirmed in class: does each of us have a guardian angel, and, if so, were they fulfilling their function if their 'charge' died or was severely injured?

"I know this all sounds weird, but I should understand more in time, like what forms angels take, where they live or stay, who assigns their tasks, etc.

"Bob, I suppose you can consider me an angel, providing comfort and serving as a messenger to you! Well, maybe I am!"

"Oh, my dearest Blanchie, if ever there was an angel, you are one!"

twenty three

Relationships in Heaven

"That's so sweet, Bob; you are an angel, too!

"Say, you and I often talked about relationships in heaven."

"Oh, on that subject, Blanchie, before I forget, I've been wanting to ask you—have you seen Julie? She was truly a pain in so many people's sides…and other body parts!"

"Ah, yes, Bob…Julie! Yes, remember she died I guess three years ago, and she's here. I spoke with her a week ago on the phone (I'll explain communicating in Heaven later). She still lives in Fresno with her husband, Ike, who, as you probably recall, used to be her doormat! What a difference Heaven makes in one's life and personality! Just the other day, here in Heaven with me, she was gracious, witty, and genuine. I had to pinch myself! She apologized for making life unpleasant for you, me, and just about anyone she ever came in contact with. She wants us to get together before and after you arrive to Heaven! I thought my jaw would drop!

"Well, this is just one of billions of examples of people who had lives of conflict on Earth but not in Heaven; another aspect of Heaven, I guess you might say, is to 'forgive and forget.' Most of the time, bad relationships on Earth are corrected in Heaven, but exceptions can include victims of brutal crimes, their families, and the perpetrators of the crimes.

"Bob, on this subject, I would like you to reconsider your relationship with your dad. He has made amends with your mom and has a great relationship with Stevie and Bobby. He told me that he deeply regrets his poor relationships with your mom and you, and that he would like to tell you this and start over."

"I hear you, Honey, and I appreciate you gently nudging me on this issue instead of hitting me over the head with a sledgehammer! This is a very emotional issue for me! Know that I'm thinking about it."

"I know, Bob!

"Well, moving on, I mentioned before the tribunal that was held here in Heaven in which Hitler and his minions were transported from various HPs to face their victims—so I'd say that, yes, victims and perpetrators can, in fact, have some kind of contact here in Heaven if the perpetrator is in Hell. So, I suppose I would be wrong if I said that Heaven is one hundred percent happiness and pain free, both emotionally and physically. I'm going to follow up on this very interesting subject!

"Here in Heaven, another interesting victim/perpetrator relationship has been the Catholic Church and victims during the Inquisition and the sex-abuse cases of the past seventy-five or so years, to name but a small fraction of the incidents. There have been steps to recognize the Church's involvement in both, and I'll be interested what the final outcome is, if any. So, to a large degree, earthly problems and joys follow on to Heaven; this makes perfect sense if Heaven is a parallel universe. Remember on our bench how we discussed the importance of living a responsible life on Earth for this same reason?

"To make a long story short, most bad relationships on Earth seem to be fixed in Heaven, or at least resolved to some degree. As in the case of different countries, we're really talking about personal relationships between heads of state that are also fixed, and that translate into whole countries getting along with one another. Again, I don't know why or how this happens."

"Blanchie, on this general subject, I'm curious about another of our topics, you remember, of former spouses in Heaven."

"Ah, yes, Bob. I forgot to tell you, but two days ago I spoke with Jack—you remember, our neighbor five houses down who was married three times? Yes, he's here! Well, he and his second wife, Maryann, are back together. They divorced while on Earth. This gets to your point, well, our point, that we discussed over the years: what happens to couples, married or not, who divorce, break up, or are widowed? Can they choose who to live with in Heaven, and if so, are there bad feelings among the former spouses and significant others? From what I've seen, there do not seem to be any bad feelings in these scenarios. Why? I dunno—I guess it's a Heaven thing!"

"Yes, Blanchie, please keep on this subject. Remember how it fascinated us on our bench?"

"Yes, it did, Bob! You know, come to think about it, in one of our classes, this subject was discussed. Just as in this case, former spouses choose to get back together in Heaven, or not, with no jealousy issues among former wives, husbands, girlfriends, and boyfriends. People are free to date and marry in Heaven, too, including same-sex couples, with no ill feelings on anyone's part. I guess this validates my initial observation of Heaven: it's basically the same as living on Earth, only nearly perfect!"

"Same-sex couples in Heaven…I remember we discussed this a lot, too, Honey. So, what is the Catholic Church's stance on this issue in Heaven?"

"Well, Bob, it appears that the Catholic Church is still opposed to same-sex marriages, but, as on Earth, same-sex couples abound here in Heaven, so that—drumroll, please—it appears that being homosexual does not send someone to Hell!"

"Earlier you made some kind of reference to Heaven's 'entry requirements.' From what I can see, they seem to be very liberal, so take the hint and be a bad boy for once! On second thought, don't you dare!"

"Ha, Blanchie, this is one old dog that couldn't learn that new trick!"

"Okay, let me clear my throat and get through this next subject as fast as I can! We talked many, many times about sex in Heaven, remember? Yes, there is sex in Heaven, but women cannot become pregnant, just as no one can die. As I alluded to a second ago, sex among the same gender happens, too, and is very common, albeit not approved, of course, by the Catholic Church. And no, Bob, I don't know how this comes to be, but, well, you know the rest…I'm on it!"

"Blanchie, while we're both blushing, let's address a topic we discussed maybe just a few times. So spouses know if their partner cheated on them while on Earth, and can spouses in Heaven see their living spouses on Earth having sex with a new partner?"

"Why, Bob Fisher! You little rascal, you! Do you maybe have something to tell me?"

"Oh, cut it out, Blanchie. You know I don't!"

"I know, silly Bob. Just pullin' your leg!

"This subject is as awkward as having 'the talk' with our kids, which, I dare say, neither of us had with our parents or with our kids!

"I remember those questions! The answer to both questions seems to be no. Another thing, Bob—it seems that secrets really do go with someone to the grave! There is no interest in Heaven in knowing if one's partner was unfaithful or did other wrong things while on Earth.

"Okay, Bob, continuing sorta on the subject of relationships in Heaven, residents find out about happenings in our families and circles of friends through this social media network on Heaven's Internet called Catch Up, very similar to Facebook. The logo is a red ketchup bottle... get it, Mr. Notorious Punster? One uses Catch Up to know what's going on with family and friends on Earth, including deaths. The difference from Facebook, though, is that Catch Up is only one-way and cannot be used to communicate with anyone on Earth. And, no, I don't know how it works!

"Oh, silly Bob, why am I mentioning this to you? You could never even spell Facebook, let alone use it!"

"Ha, Blanchie. I resemble that! I never needed to use Facebook because you and the kids told me what was going on and sent my greetings to everyone. You know that I'm old school, and you were always tuned in to young people things and the latest technology!"

"I know, Bob. I was always the yin, and you were always the yang... LOL, as the young people say!

"Well, we also have the Heaven News Network, HNN, covering only positive news in Heaven. The channels you and I watched most of our lives on Earth are not here. Just as one on Earth has no idea what goes on in Heaven, it's the same here; we have no real idea what's happening on Earth except for news of family and friends via Catch Up.

"By the way, Bob, I'm still trying to answer the question of who or what decides who comes to Heaven or goes to Hell, and what this process is.

"Oh, Bob, get this: This Friday, all of us will meet some of our relatives from previous generations! This is a yearly event, so it looks like I died just in time! I understand that it will be relatives from up to about two hundred years prior that will be together, and, in our case, everyone will meet just thirty feet from our bench at Cuesta Park! Don't ask me how this will happen, especially how they will travel here and back! I don't know where everyone is going to stay, but I can't worry about that, as there is a committee that handles each person's reunion. I think the event will be catered, and that's a relief!

"I have so many questions to ask my relatives and yours, most of whom I only know by name, like Aunt Margaret and Aunt Gertie on my mother's side, and your Dad's family that I never met, especially his parents from Illinois! I do hope your family can make it! I'll know in a few days!

"And Bob, I'm so hoping that your grandfather, Carl Fisher, attends, too, coming from Germany!"

"Wow, Blanchie! I can't even imagine this reunion or how it will be arranged! I'm sure that everyone else will be nervous, too, so this should be of some comfort! I'll be looking forward to hearing about it, especially everything about my dad's family! I assume that my dad will attend. It should be interesting to see what he says."

"Well, Bob, I think it will go just fine. Maybe I detect a note of skepticism on your part regarding your dad? Believe me, Bob, he has changed!

"Well, Bob, getting back on track, another significant relationship that is fixed here in Heaven is our relationship with Mother Earth. Imagine a world free of pollution and forest devastation! Here it is!

"Remember the creek that ran next to the Old Mission on Earth? Take a look at it, and when you come to Heaven, you'll see the same creek, only pristine! The same goes with the rivers, oceans, lakes, and rainforests worldwide—all immaculate and intact! Oh, Bob, Heaven is so beautiful, more so than you and I ever saw on Earth or could have imagined! This reminds me of when we would hear people comment that so many wonders of nature, like a beautiful sunset or waterfall or snow-covered mountain peaks, could only be the work of God. Well, maybe, and this gets us back to the discussions we had about God versus a random, natural reason for everything that happens—in other words, evolution versus creationism, nature versus God.

"And Bob, we learned that our Earth is the only planet with any form of human, animal, and plant life in the entire universe! One of the Mars robots discovered many interesting things, but evidence of life was not one of them. We have been told that, in all of the seemingly countless galaxies and universes, no evidence of life exists, not even with these sophisticated radio telescopes. This issue, again, is directly tied to the same issues of evolution, or the big bang theory, and creationism."

"I dunno, Blanchie, the Mars robot and many high-powered, telescopic photos seem to suggest that there at least used to be life on other planets. Please keep 'digging!'"

"Oh, dear Bob, I will keep 'digging' as you say, but again I'm sorry to say that this is not a popular issue, at least the evolution issue."

twenty four

World Peace in Heaven

"Say, Blanchie, remember one of the topics we discussed all the time, about if there would finally be world peace in Heaven? What have you learned? How can so many countries, so many people, all of a sudden get along? What changes in Heaven to make this happen, and why? Who allows this change?"

"And...yes, yes, yes, Bob, one of the first things I was told even before our classes began was that this is a heaven of world peace! Remember that this is a parallel Earth, with the same countries that one knows when they are living on Earth. Heaven is Earth absent war, corruption, hate, and jealousy! So, if you want to know what Heaven is like in other religions, I guess all you have to do is travel and talk to people!

"In one of our classes, we were reminded that most religions' goals included world peace while on their former Earth, but because of things unrelated to religion, like self-interest, politics, and jealousy, most religions, throughout the years, lost sight and track of world peace. This has led to a snowball effect for thousands of years of stubbornness, bad feelings, war, and oppression, making world peace unattainable. I guess, from a religious point of view, world turmoil can be said to be a byproduct of sin.

"Every night I see the news about Earth on Heaven News Network, or HNN, but there is only happy and positive news! Last night they reported on a world summit held in Geneva attended by representatives from North and South Korea, Iran and Israel, and most of the world's nations! The subjects focused on maintaining good relationships between all countries worldwide."

"Okay, Blanchie, but do they report on the Dodgers when they lose?"

"Silly Bob, of course!

"Now, you may ask, why is this a crime-and-war-free Heaven? Ultimately, I don't know. I guess it's part and parcel of Heaven itself being what it is!"

twenty five

Travelling in Heaven

"Understood, Detective Blanchie! Well, this next area we didn't discuss as much as so many others, but how does one travel in Heaven? Can one order flights and hotels online, through, say, Expedia, Travelocity, etc.? Does one pay with money?"

"Ah, Bob, you ask a good question! Well, remember that this is a parallel Earth, which means it's almost exactly like when one lived on it before going to Heaven.

"Again, in Heaven, as I mentioned before, there is no money. Everything is available to everyone, and people come back to work just for the satisfaction of working. Don't ask me how all this is—it just is! Not even our instructors knew! I'll have to think about what I'll want to do as soon as things settle down. Maybe I'll continue to do what I did for seventy-one years—take care of you!"

"Hey, Blanchie, that sounds like a great idea!"

"Anyway, in Heaven, we have all the services we had on Earth: the same airlines and local, national, and international supermarkets, like Skollary's and Walmart. If you have a plumbing problem, you can still call your national chain or local plumber. In my case, I'll call Hiram, who passed away six years ago, and who, by the way, I saw downtown at the clock tower in front of the courthouse three days ago. He sends his regards!

"You can have a car if you want. All the same roads and highways are still here! You're going to ask about accidents, I'm sure. Yes, there are still accidents, and people get hurt, but no one dies! Think about it: you can't die twice! Drivers are very courteous and obey the law, at least in the

United States, and I'm told this is true worldwide. In the United States, Heaven has ninety-five percent fewer accidents than on Earth, and the statistic Heaven-wide is also excellent! And guess what, Bob? There is no road rage!"

"Oh, Blanchie, sorry to interrupt you, but I have to ask the same question you and I asked for so many years: Why, why is none of this known on Earth, like Heaven as a parallel universe, more information about the Holy Trinity, Mary, the saints, angels, the devil, Hell, bad relationships healed, and everything we used to discuss on our bench? Wouldn't it lead to us humans acting more humane on Earth, knowing that things will be so much better in Heaven? Why has most of this information been so mysterious? No one, regardless of their religion, or lack thereof, should be in the dark about the afterlife. If we knew more about it here on Earth, we would all treat each other much better as individuals and nations, and our environment would be better off. We would all be so much happier!"

"Amen to that, Bob! Yes, you and I asked these 'why' questions so many times!

"Okay, where were we…ah, yes, travel! The last airline crash was sixty years ago, but, again, no one died. In Heaven, the airlines and their maintenance staffs are free of greed, jealousy, and motives to undermine service and safety, to include poor work ethics. As in all other areas of life, pilots, mechanics, and all support staff and administration have chosen to return to what they did on Earth, or, in many cases, to learn new careers.

"The same goes for anyone else in Heaven: If they want to return to their former line of work, or start in something new, they may do so. Or they can elect to stay retired and go fishing! They can always return to work. After all, they have all eternity!

"Oh, silly Bob, I can't wait to travel and explore Heaven with you! Everyone I've talked to, including Stevie, Bobby, our parents, and our grandparents, have travelled to some degree and have described to me the complete safety, lack of worries, and—get this, dear Bob—free hotels, that they have experienced while travelling here in Heaven."

twenty six

Pets in Heaven

"Oh, Blanchie, moving along to another elephant in the room, I hesitate to bring up this subject, because it's so emotional for you and me. I guess I'll just come out and—"

"Bob, yes, we see our pets again! Every night I am welcomed with open paws by Hank, our black lab from fifty years ago; Sandy, our calico cat; and her offspring, Willie, Flyball, and Scully, from forty years ago. Remember how we gave them baseball names? Also, remember our cat Babe; Oliver our cavalier King Charles spaniel; and, of course, our sweet golden retriever, Alexa, and american bulldog, Roxie!"

"Oh, Blanchie, I knew it, I knew it, I just did! Remember we always said that we would see our family members again and that, therefore, it made sense that we'd see our pet family members, too? Yes! Oh, please give each of them a big, big hug for me, and tell them how much I love them and how much I've missed them!"

"Yes, silly Bob! They're all here and as sweet as ever! Our older pets, and even our newer ones, are one of the things that makes Heaven so happy and fun! Sandy sleeps with me in our bed as she did for so many years! The best part is that they all get along, which makes sense, based on the same phenomenon among humans in Heaven!

"And the best part, Bob...get this: they will be with us for all eternity, too!

"Bob, we also used to discuss the purpose of pets on Earth. From a religious point of view, we said that God put them on Earth to give us love, but we never quite figured out the scientific reason except to say

105

that they, like us humans, evolved as did all animal life, including humans, and simply existed while we took advantage of their loyal natures and unconditionally loving spirits! I think we believed in a combination of both versions!

"Well, Bob, on that note, I'm gonna get going to class! Did I tell you that graduation—well, our last day of classes, is in two days?"

"Ha, Blanchie! Are you going to be the class valedictorian and give a rebel speech, questioning the creationism-versus-evolution theories?"

"Listen, your Royal Silliness, there won't be anything like that, not even a certificate! And the best news is that most of us in our class will continue to see each other every day! Well, we'll talk tomorrow at seven a.m. as usual, okay? I love you so much, Bob!"

"Me, too, my dearest Blanchie. Please give all of our human and pet family my love and lots of hugs!"

"Will do, Bob. Now, let me get to class. I love you!"

"I love you too, Blanchie; we'll talk in the morning!"

twenty seven

Patching Things Up

"Good morning, Blanchie! I love you! How's your Pete's coffee, and what should we discuss this morning?"

"Good morning to you, too, my dearest Bob, and I love you too! I'm glad you used the words 'should discuss,' because I have just the topic. And he's sitting right next to me!"

"Oh, uh, Blanchie, I just don't know; are you talking about…?"

"Bobby? Bobby? Is this really you? Bobby? Are you there?"

"Yes, Dad, I'm here."

"Oh, Bobby, this is very awkward for me. I asked your mother to be here with me, and she said that it would be better for you and me to speak alone. Even Blanche has gone into another room to give us privacy."

"Okay, Dad."

"Bobby, where do I start? I was a miserable husband, father, grandfather, and human being. I showed very little financial support and no love to your mother or to you, and I made your lives so, so unhappy.

"I don't remember ever saying 'I love you' to either of you. I don't remember ever even hugging you, taking you fishing, watching just one of your youth baseball games, attending any of your school functions or graduations, or just doing things that normal fathers and sons do.

"And we didn't get a chance to make amends or to say good-bye before I died. Bobby…Bobby, are you still there?"

"Yes, Dad, I'm still here."

"I robbed you of so much love and so many experiences that we could have had together during your youth and adulthood. Thanks to your mother, she made up for all my failures, taking you to the movies, to the beach, to church, to Grammie Poke's house for the holidays and summers, and so many other places. She also served as grandfather to Johnny, Timothy, and Mary. She might have told you that we have made amends. Oh, Bobby, I was so mean to her, but, then, again, you know that—you were there."

"Dad, I think—"

"Bobby, I love you, and I'm so, so heartfully sorry! There, I said it—better late than never. Please relay my love to Johnny, Timothy, Mary, and all of my grand-, great-, and great-great-grandkids. I was the worst grandfather in the history of grandfathers. Please tell them that I'll make up for this in the next life!

"Bobby, can you forgive me...May I be your father? Bobby, are you still there?"

"Uh, yes, Dad, I, uh, I'm here."

"Bobby, don't cry, 'cause you'll make me cry, too...Oh, what the hell, let's both have a good cry! Blanchie, you might as well come join in the cry fest. I can see you through the crack in the door!"

"Oh, Bob, I hope you don't mind. I thought it was the right time!"

"You're right, Blanchie; it was the right time!

"Dad, I have thought about this moment all my life—what I would say to you when we met in Heaven and how I would feel. I guess I got caught a little off guard just now, but I'll speak from the heart: Dad, I love you too, and I forgive you! Have you seen the movie *Field of Dreams,* where the grown man has a catch with his dad who came back to life on the baseball field? Yes, please be my father, and could we someday have that catch?"

"Of course, son, of course. I'd love that! I guess I never told you that I played a little baseball in SLO when it first came out around 1915! I mostly played third base."

"No, Dad, you didn't. Speaking of catching, there's a lot of catching up to do for you and me! Blanchie will arrange for us to talk often like this, okay?"

"I'll love that, son! Oh, and I guess there's a first time for everything. I love you, Bobby!"

"I love you too, Dad!"

"Oh Bob, we're all bawling like babies: me, Speeder, Bobby Jr., and Stevie! Bob, welcome to the 'made amends club'!"

"Bobby, this is Speeder. I'm an emotional wreck, as are the rest of us! We all send you our love, and we so look forward to your arrival! Please give our love also to Johnny, Timothy, Mary, and all our greats and great-greats!"

"Wow, Bob, this has been the most emotional day of my life! I'm so happy that you and your Dad have finally reconciled! I think we all need a break, so we'll talk in the morning, okay? I love you so much, and I'm so proud of you!

"Before I forget, tomorrow is graduation. But we can talk as usual because the graduation is at nine a.m., just like my classes."

"Great, Blanchie, and thank you for arranging this little meeting with Dad. You always had a great sense of timing and what is the right thing to do! Sleep tight. I love you so much, too, and we'll talk in the morning, graduate!"

twenty eight

Blanchie's Graduation

"Good morning, Blanchie! Because this morning is special, I went to Pete's and got me one of those Frappuccino drinks. I'm sure you're kinda glad to settle back into some kind of routine at home, and maybe we can talk a little longer in the morning!

"Uh, Blanchie? Blanchie, are you there? Earth to Blanchie! Hm. Well, I guess you had to get to graduation a little earlier than usual. I'll wait a few more minutes. If I don't hear from you, I'll just come back tomorrow morning! I love you so much!"

Meanwhile, back in Heaven, the graduation begins...

"Ladies and gentlemen, please be seated. Today is the last day of orientation, and we hope that it has helped you to transition a little easier into your new life here in Heaven. We make ourselves available every day for your questions, as we know we couldn't address all of them in this short time.

"Blanche Fisher, many here, myself included, knew you for most of your life in SLO, and most of us were aware of your daily morning chats with Bob as you sat on your park bench for, I guess, all of your married life, pondering many tough questions about religion. I know, too, that you have tried so hard to get answers to your biggest questions in your short stay here in Heaven. Heck, you asked so many! I encourage you to keep asking, as even I, after twenty years in Heaven, find that many answers are still hard to find!

"Now, before we disband, I just got word of our newest resident, who arrived not even an hour ago! He is so new that I don't know who he is!

"Let's give a warm round of applause to our newest member of Heaven. Please come forward!"

"Bob? Bob?"

"Blanchie? Oh, my God…Blanchie? Is that you? Where are you?"

"Bob? Bob! Oh, Bob…I can't believe it! Here I am!"

"Blanchie, I can't see you. I'm so nervous, and I don't know if I can walk to you. My knees feel like Jell-O!"

"Hang on, Bob, I'm coming! Get ready for the biggest kiss of your life, or, well, of your afterlife!"

As Blanchie runs over to Bob in the rear of the classroom, the entire class and instructors turn and erupt in a standing ovation! There's not a dry eye to be seen!

"Bob, I love you so much!"

"Oh, Blanchie, I love you so much, too! Is this real? Am I dreaming? Is this, is this—?"

"Yes, silly Bob, you've made it. Welcome to Heaven!"

"This is so, so, I can't believe it! Oh, Blanchie, you look maybe thirty-ish?"

"So do you, Bob, so do you! Here, come look at yourself in the bathroom mirror. Go on, take a look!"

"Blanchie…Blanchie! I'm young again! My shoulders…my shoulders don't hurt anymore!"

"I told you, Bob; everything here in Heaven is fixed from how you knew it on Earth! Now, come over here and give me another hug and kiss!

"Now, how's about we go sit on our bench?"

"Ha, I was just sitting on it…I think…next thing, I'm here!"

"But, you know, Blanchie, that idea sounds so…so…heavenly! What is it I used to say?"

"'Let's go, Blanchie. Our bench awaiteth. Grab your coffee!'"

31016014R00074

Made in the USA
Charleston, SC
01 July 2014